# AFRICA
## ON MY MIND

## Reflections Of My Second Trip

By
Atlantis Tye Browder
With
Anthony T. Browder

The Institute of Karmic Guidance
Washington, D.C.

AFRICA ON MY MIND
Reflections Of My Second Trip

By
Atlantis Tye Browder
With
Anthony T. Browder

Published by
The Institute of Karmic Guidance
P.O. Box 73025
Washington, D.C.  20056
(301) 853-2465 voice
(301) 853-7916 fax

Cover Illustration:  Kevin Watson
Publication Layout & Design: Tony Browder

Library of Congress Catalog Card Number: 95-095215

ISBN: 0-924944-08-0
Paperback/ $11.99

ISBN: 0-924944-09-9
Hardcover/ $24.99

1st Printing
November, 1995

Printing:  International Graphics/Beltsville, Maryland

# Dedication

This work is dedicated to our respective grandmothers
Anne E. Browder and Mary E. Walker.
We thank you for making our lives whole.


A special dedication is extended to
the millions of African families that were destroyed
because of the greed and hatred of others.
We will always remember you.

# Acknowledgments

We would like to express our thanks to our family for their love and support. With special thanks to our grandmother/mother, Anne, for her editorial expertise and Auntie Rosie for her evaluation of the manuscript.

Special acknowledgment must be given to Haile Gerima and James Boyce for allowing us to use the photographs from the movie *Sankofa* which appear on pages 40 and 41. We also would like to thank Michael Graham-Stewart for providing the photograph on page 45. As usual, we must also thank our brother Phil Collins for continuing to supply us with photographs for all of our publications.

In addition, we would like to thank Kevin Watson for the wonderful portrait that graces our cover and Marcus Murga for his creative illustrations. We are also eternally grateful to Sharon Smith for giving us the idea to write our first book -- six years ago.

# About the Cover

It is not forbidden to return to the past to
reclaim something which has been forgotten. You can
always correct your mistakes.
                                    - *A Ghanaian proverb*

### "Child of Africa"

The portrait of Atlantis shows her holding the staff of a
linguist which is topped with the symbol of the *Sankofa Bird*.
The Sankofa Bird represents the spirit of the proverb written
above. A linguist is the spokesperson of a king, and is
responsible for putting the chief's whispers into poetic and
eloquent language.

The Ashanti stool upon which Atlantis sits is carved with
the Adinkra symbol *Gye Nayme* which means, "except God."
It serves as a reminder that we may consider ourselves more
important than anything or anybody...*except God*. There is a
higher source to which we all must answer.

The staff, stool and Kente cloth are representations of
cultural traditions which have existed in Ghana for
hundreds of years. Their memories live within the soul of
each child of Africa.

Illustrated By
Kevin Watson, Artattack
1-800-626-0097

Concept and Cover Design By
Tony Browder, IKG

# Table of Contents

# Foreword

I am honored that Tony and Atlantis have asked me to write the foreword to their second book. This project, part of a continuing series of books, is a very special gift to the Pan-Afrikan community. It demonstrates to us what can and must come from our relationships. In this case, the very special relationship between an Afrikan parent and child -- a father and his daughter. This particular aspect of the book is significant because the healing process which must take place among our people will only happen through the experience of connectedness; through intergenerational nurturing and teaching. It is through such relationships that we once learned our identity, our responsibility and our place in a system of accountability. We must now rebuild these relationships consciously through Afrikan-centered work and creativity. All too often, we who in adulthood have discovered so late the power of Afrikan self-knowledge, have failed to pass that discovery on to our children. Without this knowledge, our children grow up in ignorance as we did and fail to build self-determining institutions as we have.

This book is a model of the fundamental relationship between parent and child which is symbolic of Afrika as the "parent" and we in the Afrikan Diaspora as the "child returning home." The theme of the book is *Sankofa*; going back to move forward: Reconnecting, rebuilding relationships with who we are.

The information about West Afrika is presented in a clear straight-forward manner, accessible to anyone who can read it or hear its text. Yet in its simplicity, there is a depth of understanding and accuracy which cannot fail to effect the consciousness of every Afrikan person it touches.

Tony helps Atlantis to process the experience of the trip -- "the return home" -- by patiently discussing with her the importance of history and the relationship of personal history to cultural history for Afrikan people. In this way their dialogue, inspired by the trip, generates information about Afrikan Diasporic culture, and its origins, and raises important issues, such as the effect of European-controlled media on the minds of our youth. Young people can then make the connection between the European Slave Trade in Afrikan lives and contemporary European-American methods of controlling Afrikan minds. Through Atlantis' eyes, her responses to what she experiences, and her questions, she and other young Afrikans in America and elsewhere are exposed to information which is a missing piece of the puzzle of their own self-definition. Our children must have this sense of identity if they are to determine their own future and define reality for themselves in the interests of their people.

Atlantis' book tells part of the story of the enslavement of Afrikan people and its historical significance; information which far too many of our people lack and others are reluctant to discuss. The book exposes a phenomenon -- the rape of Afrika, the stealing of her children, and their definition as "property" which we know of as the *Maafa* (an act of disconnection). This story is crucial because until we and our children are able to truthfully confront the *Maafa* and all that it means, we will not reconnect with the source of our cultural energy (*Sankofa*).

The cooperative family work of Tony and Atlantis Browder is helping to break the cycle of ignorance and cultural discontinuity which has plagued Afrikan people. It should be given to all Afrikan children and families in the Diaspora and on the Continent. It is to be read and spread and celebrated.

Medasi
("Thank you")

Marimba Ani

# Preface

Before reading this book it would be helpful to familiarize yourself with specific concepts. In our attempt to center ourselves within a framework that is historically and culturally African centered, we have chosen to:

1. Use maps of Africa that are based upon the *Peters Projection.*
2. Use references to people based upon ethnicity (African and European), as opposed to color (black and white). When the terms *black* and *white* are used, they are not capitalized.
3. Refer to the human beings who were sold into slavery in the New World as *enslaved Africans* and not *slaves*.
4. Refer to the process of enslaving Africans in the New World as the *European Slave Trade.*
5. Refer to the period of the European Slave Trade and the enslavement of African people (1444-1870) as the *Maafa.* This African word references the *great disaster* which befell Africans when they were stolen from their homeland and *dispersed* throughout the West.
6. Reevaluate the numbers of Africans who survived the Middle Passage. After consulting numerous sources, we were advised to use a conservative estimate of 50 million to represent the number of Africans brought to the New World.

While writing this book it was our desire to help put a face on the nameless victims of the Maafa. When you look into the eyes of the Africans depicted on these pages and read their history, we hope that you will remember their pain, suffering and triumphs. We hope that you will discuss the relevancy of their history with your family, friends and classmates.

In the story *Roots*, Alex Haley told us that Kunta Kinte was stolen while searching for wood with which to make a drum -- and he never saw his family again. This act was repeated thousands of times over hundreds of years and millions of families were destroyed, in Africa and in the Americas. We must never forget or trivialize this human tragedy.

Historian, Dr. John Henrik Clarke informs us that, "All history is a current event." We are aware that slavery still exists in America and millions of families continue to be destroyed. They are destroyed by people who are slaves to *drug addiction, violence, crime, poverty and ignorance.* These are all manifestations of *mental slavery.*

Dr. Asa Hilliard, a historian and educational psychologist, suggests that mental slavery is sometimes worse than physical bondage. This is because the mental slave is "self contained" and, while believing that they are free to do as they please, they are active participants in their continued enslavement.

Our salvation lies in remembering the lessons of Dr. Clarke and others who teach us that it is impossible to enslave people who are "historically conscious." Our objective is to awaken our consciousness, study our history, record it and pass it on to others. We trust that our actions will please our ancestors and benefit those who will walk in our footsteps.

# Authors' Introduction

It seems like ages ago when my father and I co-authored our book entitled *My First Trip To Africa.* That was back in 1991, when I was about eight and a half years old.

*My First Trip To Africa* was the journey that I made to Egypt with my father who is a lecturer and a writer. He also takes people on study tours and teaches them about African History.

During my trip to Egypt, in 1989, I was asked by someone in our group what I wanted to be when I grew up. I remember telling them that I wanted to be a lecturer like my father, and that he would tell me what to say and I would tell others.

Since writing my first book, that's exactly what I've been doing. I have traveled all over the United States and I have shared my experiences with thousands of youths and adults. People like what I have to say, but I am amazed by how little they know about Africa.

I'm usually asked questions like, "Do Africans wear clothes like us?" Or "Do African people live in houses and eat food?" Because most people have never visited Africa, they believe that all the terrible things they read in the newspaper or see on TV are happening all over Africa. I tell people that that is not true.

I hope when people read my books they will begin to understand that there are many beautiful things in Africa too. I want people to understand that Africa is not a country. Africa is the second largest continent on earth and is three times the size of the United States.

Africa is made up of 53 countries, and I have been privileged to visit five of them. I hope to visit many more countries in the future. I also plan to continue sharing my reflections of Africa with you, and I hope you will continue to learn from them.

Atlantis Tye Browder

Ever since my daughter was a young child, I have taken the initiative to teach her about Africa. We've attended numerous lectures, met famous historians, and traveled extensively. I've done this because my introduction to African history and culture didn't begin until I was in my mid 20's. I wanted to give Atlantis an earlier start in life.

Teaching my daughter about Africa has been beneficial to her, to me, and countless others. Since writing our first book, I have spoken with many parents who have told me of the profound impact *My First Trip To Africa* has had on their children.

There are two stories which stand out most in my mind. The first story involved a woman from Bowie, Maryland who had given a copy of my daughter's book to her ten year old son. The young boy wrote a book report entitled "My First Trip To Africa" and submitted it to his 5th grade teacher. The teacher reprimanded the child -- in front of his classmates -- and told them that the book report was unacceptable because it said that Egypt was in Africa.

When the boy's mother learned of this incident, she promptly demanded a meeting with her son's teacher and the school principal. She gave them both a history and a geography lesson. She also insisted that her son's teacher apologize to him in the presence of his classmates.

The second story was about an African male, his African American wife, and their seven year old daughter. The father told me that he had been trying to interest his daughter in traveling to Nigeria with him to visit her grandparents. She steadfastly refused to go. When the young child was about five years old, she finally told her father that she was afraid to visit Africa because she thought that she would be eaten by wild animals. Despite reassurances to the contrary, the young girl refused to travel to Africa.

One day the father gave his daughter a copy of my daughter's book. She read the first sentence which said, "I was seven years old when I made my first trip to Africa." The child turned to her father and said, "She was seven years old when she went to Africa, I'm seven years old, I want to go to Africa!" The father was excited beyond belief to have discovered that all it took to turn his daughter around was to see Africa through the favorable eyes of someone closer to her own age.

These two stories underscore the many misconceptions that children and adults have about Africa, Africans and African history. My daughter and I are committed to spreading the good news about our heritage, and giving Africans throughout the world reasons to feel proud. We hope that you will appreciate our efforts.

Anthony T. Browder

# AFRICA

## ON MY MIND

## Reflections Of My Second Trip

Chapter 1

# My Journey to West Africa

I don't remember the exact day that my father asked me if I wanted to go to West Africa, but I immediately said yes. It had been four years since I first visited Africa. In 1991 my father and I co-authored *"My First Trip To Africa"* which chronicles the trip we made to Egypt in 1989.

On of my most memorable moments, during my first trip to Africa, was when we visited the Temple of Karnak. I posed for a picture while sitting on the lap of a statue of Amenhotep II.

I looked forward to traveling to West Africa because of the exciting time I had in Egypt. My father and I also looked forward to another opportunity to write about my travels. This time, instead of writing about Egypt, we would write about life in four West African countries.

We traveled to the West African nations of *Senegal* (sehn uh GAWL), *The Gambia, Ghana,* and *Cote d'Ivoire* (KOHT D' VOIR), which in English means *Ivory Coast*. In preparation for our trip we had to get travel visas from each of the African embassies, and inoculations against yellow fever and tetanus. We also had to take a malaria tablet once a week, beginning two weeks before the trip, the two weeks during the trip, and for two weeks after we returned home.

We were told to take these health precautions so that we wouldn't become ill during our trip. Our travel agent also advised us to drink only bottled water because our bodies were not used to the bacteria in the water of the countries that we would be visiting. They didn't want to risk any of us getting sick and ruining our trip.

On Wednesday, July 21, 1993, my grandmother, father, and three other people began the first part of our journey. Mr. Abdullah Yusef, a friend of my father's, drove us from Washington, D.C. to J.F.K. Airport in New York City where we would catch our overseas flight. The drive took about five hours. When we arrived at J.F.K. Airport we met up with 19 other people who continued the journey with us to West Africa.

Three of the people on this trip had traveled to Egypt with us in 1989 and it was good to see them again. The others in our group had traveled from Massachusetts, Colorado, Georgia, California, Michigan, North Carolina, New York, and Florida. We all introduced ourselves and waited excitedly for our evening departure to *Dakar* (dah KAHR), Senegal.

# SENEGAL

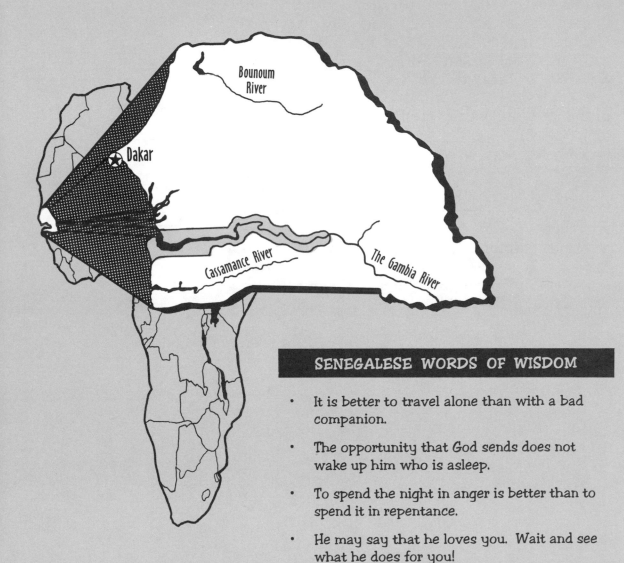

Bounoum River

★ Dakar

Cassamance River

The Gambia River

## SENEGALESE WORDS OF WISDOM

- It is better to travel alone than with a bad companion.

- The opportunity that God sends does not wake up him who is asleep.

- To spend the night in anger is better than to spend it in repentance.

- He may say that he loves you. Wait and see what he does for you!

## Senegal

<u>Official Name:</u> Republique du Senegal
<u>Area:</u> 76,000 sq. mi. /196,840 sq. km.
<u>Population:</u> 7,945,267
<u>Capital City:</u> Dakar

<u>Colonized By:</u> France (1882-1960)
<u>Name during Colonial Times:</u> Senegal
<u>National Language(s):</u> French; Wolof, Fulani
<u>National Religion(s):</u> Muslim, Christian, Traditional

# Senegal

We left J.F.K. International Airport for Senegal late Wednesday evening. We flew for seven hours and traveled a distance of approximately 3,820 miles (6,112 kilometers). Our flight arrived in Dakar, the capital of Senegal, early Thursday morning on July 22nd.

Senegal is a small country on the northwest coast of Africa. It extends further west than any other country on the African continent. Senegal covers an area of 76,000 square miles (196,840 square kilometers), and is about the size of the state of South Dakota. It has a tropical climate and is composed of mostly forests.

Nearly eight million people live in Senegal. French is the official language because Senegal was colonized by France between 1882 and 1960. Most Senegalese also speak *Wolof* (Woolof) and other traditional languages, in addition to English. Many of the people we met spoke at least three languages.

Eighty-five percent of the population is Muslim. Senegal had been conquered by the Arabs hundreds of years before it was colonized by the French. The rest of the Senegalese practice Christianity or traditional African religions. One of the first lessons I learned on this trip was that whenever Africans were colonized they were forced to learn the language, customs and religion of their conquerors.

Upon our arrival in Dakar, we were transferred to our hotel which overlooked the Atlantic Ocean. Since Senegal is five hours ahead of Eastern Standard Time, some members of our group wanted to rest but

*We met many merchants on the streets and we could negotiate prices for everything we purchased.*

others couldn't wait to begin exploring the city. I was part of the latter group and as soon as we unpacked, a group of us went sightseeing.

Dakar is a very modern city which has over 1,300,000 people. The downtown area has large skyscrapers and attractive boulevards which are lined with trees on both sides. There were many open air markets where people sold food, clothing, live stock, and household items. We also saw miles and miles of beautiful beaches and cliffs that dropped 100 feet straight into the Atlantic Ocean.

Most of the Senegalese are dark complexioned and have silky smooth skin. They frequently wear traditional clothing which is extremely colorful and has many interesting patterns. Many of the men wear wide-legged pants and a loose-fitting robe which is called a boubou (BOO-ba). The women often wear brightly colored boubous and a matching head wrap. Some of their favorite foods are: rice, fried fish, chicken stew, and peanut soup.

What was really fascinating to me was the number of people I met on the street who looked like people I knew back home. The only real difference was that they spoke different languages. I learned later on that all of us were really distant relatives who had been separated by time and the Atlantic Ocean.

The Presidential Palace

*My grandmother and I posed with a presidential guard.*

# City Tour of Dakar

On Friday, July 23rd, we began our city tour of Dakar. We visited the Palace of the President which was patrolled by guards who were dressed in bright red uniforms. They were very friendly and several of us had our pictures taken with them while standing in front of the palace gates.

Since Dakar is the capital of Senegal, we saw a number of national monuments. In addition to the President's Palace we visited several parks and the National Assembly building. This part of the tour was a lot like visiting the parks, monuments and The Capitol in Washington, D.C.

Two sights which really impressed me were *Soweto (SO WAY TOE) Square* and *The University of Dakar*. Soweto Square is the sight of a monument which was built as an expression of solidarity for the people of South Africa during their struggle against *apartheid (ah PAHRT tate)*.

*Soweto Square*

*Cheikh Anta Diop
(1923 - 1986)*

The University of Dakar is Senegal's only university. It was re-named the *Cheikh Anta Diop (SHAKE An ta DEE Op) University* in honor of the great Senegalese scientist who died in 1986.

*Cheikh Anta Diop* was loved by the people of Senegal. He has been described as a multi-disciplinarian, like *Imhotep (im HO tep)*, the ancient Egyptian scientist and architect. Diop is known throughout the world for his expertise in Egyptology, nuclear physics, chemistry and linguistics. He was also a historian and politician.

Diop proved that Wolof and many other languages currently spoken in western Africa originated in ancient *Kemet (KIM et)*, the country that we now call Egypt. He also proved that the ancient Egyptians were Africans and not Europeans as some believed. Because of his brilliance, Diop was voted one of the most influential scholars in the twentieth century. We can understand why the Senegalese named their only university after him.

*Cheikh Anta Diop University*

# Tour of Goree Island

Later that afternoon we caught a ferry boat from Dakar to the small Island of *Goree* (GOR ee). Goree is the sight of the infamous slave dungeon and fort which was built by the Portuguese. The Portuguese landed on this island in 1444. They were the first Europeans to enslave and sell Africans. Over the next 426 years, millions of Africans were enslaved on this island before being sold overseas.

A visit to *Goree Island* is like a sacred pilgrimage for thousands of African Americans who go there every year. We went to see where our ancestors were imprisoned before being sold to men who shipped them thousands of miles away to South America, the Caribbean, and North America.

The journey made by enslaved Africans across the Atlantic Ocean was called the *Middle Passage*. The ordeal usually took about five to twelve weeks, and many people died along the way. When the Africans arrived in the *"New World,"* they were re-sold to European

*Auction block where enslaved Africans were sold.*

*Standing in the "Door of no return."*

plantation owners who became their enslavers. They were often brutally beaten and forced to work for the rest of their lives.

We were given a tour of the slave dungeon on Goree Island by Mr. Joseph Ndiaye (N JIA), the chief curator. He showed us the cells where hundreds of people were imprisoned while waiting for the ships which would take them across the Atlantic Ocean.

There were cells for men, there were cells for the women, and there were even cells for children. Families were separated and often herded in these dark cells for as long as three months. Many people were chained, beaten, and fed very poorly. We were told that the women and young girls were often raped by their European captors while they were at Goree Island and on the ships during the Middle Passage.

Most of the ships involved in the slave trade came from Europe. When they arrived at Goree Island, the African men, women and children were led out through a passageway called the *"Door of no return."* Many were dragged onboard the ships screaming and crying every step of the way. They were afraid because they didn't know where they were going, and they weren't sure if they would ever see their families again.

During this part of the tour many people became sad and started crying. Others got very angry. I understood how they felt. After the tour, Mr. Ndiaye took us in his office and asked us all to sign a book indicating that we had visited Goree Island. This book contained the names of hundreds of African American tourists, entertainers and politicians who had visited Goree Island before us.

People from all over the world who visit Goree Island learn of the tragedies which occurred there. Mr. Ndiaye showed us pictures

*With Mr. Ndiaye in his office.*

of *Pope John Paul II* who visited there in 1992. We were told that the pope prayed in one of the cells, and asked God to forgive the Christians and Europeans who were responsible for enslaving Africans hundreds of years ago.

As we rode the ferry back to Dakar, everyone was thinking about all they had seen on Goree Island. It was a short boat ride to the island, but our return trip seemed much longer. I can't even imagine what it would feel like to be held captive on a boat for two months and to never see my family again.

*Mr. Ndiaye's bulletin board displayed photos of Pope John Paul II, who visited Goree Island in February 1992.*

# Countryside Tour

On Saturday, July 24th, our group boarded a bus for a tour of the Senegal countryside. During the ride, my father talked to me about some of the misconceptions that most people have about Africa. One of the biggest myths is the belief that Africa is one huge jungle.

We certainly didn't see a jungle in Dakar, and driving in the countryside wasn't much different from drives in the country back home. What people call a "jungle" in Africa, is usually called a "rain forest" in other parts of the world. In fact, less than one fifth of the entire continent of Africa consists of rain forests.

Africa covers an area of 11,714,000 square miles (30,339,000 square kilometers) and is almost equally divided by the *equator*. Over two-fifths of Africa is *savanna*, or grassland. Many people call this area the *bush*. About two-fifths of Africa is desert. The *Sahara*, in northern Africa, is the world's largest desert and it covers over 3 1/2 million miles (9 million square kilometers).

During our drive through the savanna we didn't see any wild animals. That's another myth about Africa. We saw no lions or tigers, bears or gorillas. All we saw were cows, sheep and some dogs. Wild animals do exist in Africa, but only in certain areas. Wild animals can also be found in North America, South America, Europe and Asia.

We did see a lot of termite mounds while in the countryside. These termite mounds were huge like ant hills. Some may be 20 feet (six meters) high. The termites found in North America and Europe don't build mounds. They usually live underground or in trees and other pieces of wood.

**The Geographical Regions of Africa**

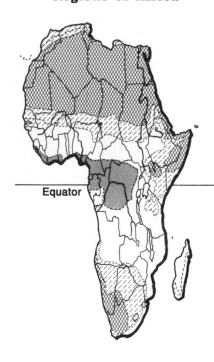

Equator

Desert

Semiarid

Savanna

Rain Forest

*Our tour bus parked under the shade of a Baobab tree.*

As we drove along the savanna we saw a number of *Baobab trees*, (BAY oh bab) which are unique to Africa. Some Baobabs are over 100 years old and are of great significance to the Senegalese. Villagers often buried their deceased family members under the Baobabs they believed to be the most spiritual. People often gathered under the Baobab for meetings and other social activities. These trees were very wide at the base and their broad branches and leaves provided shade from the hot sun.

The driver parked our bus under a Baobab tree when we stopped to visit a small village. We then walked a short distance where we met the village chief, the *elders* and other residents. The structure of the village was like that of a small town. The chief is like the mayor and the elders are his closest advisors.

In Africa, elders are highly respected because of the wisdom they have attained over the years. Because of their age, elders are considered to be closer to God and the *ancestors*. They are given much honor. Groups of elders form a *council of elders*, and they are responsible for making many of the important decisions which affect the village.

During our visit we were invited into a number of homes. We talked with many children, teenagers and adults, and took pictures with them. It's hard to believe that just 150 years ago, villages like this were raided by slave traders and entire families were enslaved. Many of them came to America. I guess that's why people in our group kept referring to the villagers as their "cousins." That was their way of saying that we were all from the same family.

*Dr. Na'im Akbar and me with our Senegalese cousins.*

On our way back to the hotel we stopped to visit an art and cultural center. While there we met a group of African American tourists who were also visiting Senegal. That tour was led by *Dr. Margaret Burroughs* who is a very famous artist and educator from Chicago, Illinois. She has been conducting tours to West Africa for over 20 years.

As it turned out, my grandmother knew Dr. Burroughs. My grandmother's family is from Chicago and Dr. Burroughs knows many of my relatives who still live there. In 1961, Dr. Burroughs and her husband, Charles, founded The *DuSable Museum of African American History*. The museum was named after *Jean Baptiste Pointe DuSable* (du SAH bul), an African American who founded the city of Chicago in 1773. Mr. and Mrs. Burroughs established the DuSable Museum because they wanted to preserve the history and culture of African Americans for future generations.

*Jean Baptiste Pointe DuSable (1745-1818)*

DuSable was born in Haiti and was probably educated in Paris. He was an explorer, fur trader, farmer and a successful business man. DuSable built a trading post on the banks of the Chicago River in 1773 and is acknowledged as the founding father of the city of Chicago, Illinois.

*Dr. Burroughs and me.*

I was introduced to Dr. Burroughs by my grandmother and we posed for a picture in front of the art center. We also saw her a few more times at our hotel in Dakar. Since our meeting, we've written letters to each other and Dr. Burroughs has encourged me to do well in school and to continue writing and drawing.

Time seemed to go by very quickly during our visit in Senegal. On our last day in Dakar I had an opportunity to go swimming with a friend from our group, while my father went to visit some friends who had recently moved back to Senegal from the U.S. After dinner, we packed and went to bed early in order to prepare for an early morning departure.

# THE GAMBIA

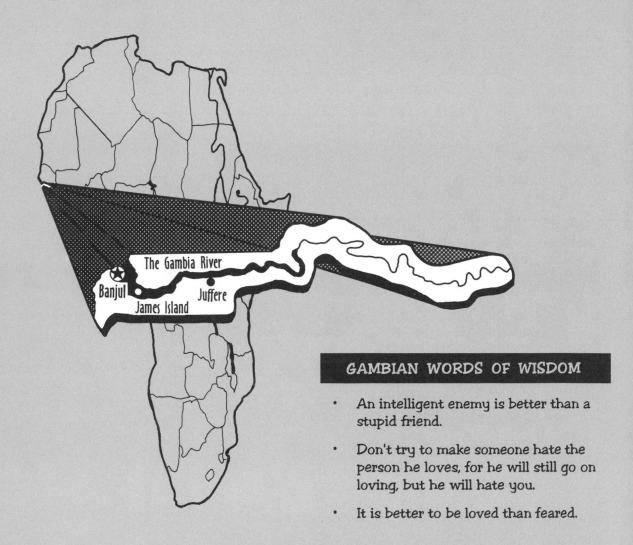

The Gambia River

Banjul
James Island
Juffere

## GAMBIAN WORDS OF WISDOM

- An intelligent enemy is better than a stupid friend.

- Don't try to make someone hate the person he loves, for he will still go on loving, but he will hate you.

- It is better to be loved than feared.

## The Gambia

**Official Name:** Republic of The Gambia
**Area:** 4,361 sq. mi. / 11,295 sq. km.
**Population:** 905,000
**Capital City:** Banjul

**Colonized By:** England (1888-1965)
**Name During Colonial Times:** Gambia
**National Language(s):** English; Mandinke, Fulani
**National Religion(s):** Muslim, Christian, Traditional

# Chapter 3

# The Gambia

On Monday, July 26, we left Dakar by bus in route to Banjul, the capital of The Gambia. The Gambia was very similar to Senegal but one major difference was the language. English is the primary language in The Gambia because that country was colonized by the British in 1888.

The geography of The Gambia is identical to that of Senegal. In fact, except for the shoreline, The Gambia is surrounded by Senegal, to the North, South and East. It is one of the smallest countries in Africa, less than half the size of the state of Vermont, and measures only 180 miles (290 kilometers) long and 15 to 30 miles (24 to 48 kilometers) wide. The Gambia is divided lengthwise by the river which also shares its name.

There are only about 905,000 people living in The Gambia. Most of them are Muslim, some are Christians and others follow traditional African religions. The Gambians and the Senegalese are actually from the same ethnic groups and speak similar African languages. They were divided by the Europeans who colonized them.

The bus ride from Dakar to Banjul took about five hours. While in route, we stopped at a very important village in The Gambia. The village is called *Juffere* (JU-fur-ay). Juffere was made famous by *Alex Haley*, the African American author of the book *"Roots."*

*Alex Haley
(1921-1992)*

Mr. Haley developed his writing abilities during his tour of duty in the U.S. Coast Guard. He was the first African American to receive a Pulitzer Prize.

He was also awarded the Spingarn medal for writing *"Roots."* Haley's first published book was *"The Autobiography of Malcolm X,"* which he co-authored in 1964.

On September 21, 1981, the city of Annapolis, Maryland erected a plaque in honor of Kunta Kinte. It reads: "To commemorate the arrival in this harbor of Kunta Kinte, immortalized by Alex Haley in *"Roots,"* and all others who came to these shores in bondage and who by their toil, character and ceaseless struggle for freedom have helped to make these United States.

A Luta Continua!

*"Roots"* is the story about how Alex Haley traced his family roots from his hometown of Henning, Tennessee, in the U.S.A., all the way to the village of Juffere in The Gambia. It took Mr. Haley ten years of research to discover the identity of his great-great-great-great-great grandfather who was named *Kunta Kinte* (KOON Ta  KIN Tay).

Kunta Kinte was born in Juffere around 1751 and was kidnapped when he was 16 years old. He was put on a slave ship in The Gambia and arrived in Annapolis, Maryland on September 29, 1767. Kunta was later sold to a farmer from Virginia who eventually changed Kunta's name to *Toby*.

Kunta missed his home dearly and he refused to accept the fact that he was to remain enslaved for the rest of his life. He ran away from the plantation several times, and each time he was captured, returned and beaten. After one failed escape attempt, his evil enslaver decided to cut off Kunta Kinte's foot so that he would never run away again. He was forced to spend the rest of his life as a cripple.

Kunta later married a woman named Bell and they had a daughter named Kizzy. Kizzy was enslaved her entire life, but her father taught her that her ancestors were once a free and proud people in Africa.

Kizzy was 16 years old when she was separated from her parents and sold to another enslaver. Years later, Kizzy had a son named George and she taught him the lessons that she learned from her father.

As a child, Alex Haley grew up hearing the stories about Kunta Kinte, his daughter, his grandson and his great grandchildren. He was deeply inspired by his family history and wanted to know more about the African who was kidnapped from his homeland. Mr. Haley spent many years researching libraries in the United States, England and Africa, searching for clues.

Alex Haley became the first African American writer to trace his roots back to Africa and to record his efforts in a book. *"Roots"* became an international best seller and was made into a television series in the U.S. Since then, the village of Juffere has become a very important tourist site in The Gambia. Juffere has about 500 residents and about 10,000 tourists visit there annually. You might say that Alex Haley helped put the village on the map.

While at Juffere, we had an opportunity to learn about the day-to-day routine of the villagers. Later, we all sat in a circle and listened to an elder storyteller, called a *griot (GREE oh)*, who gave us an oral history of the village. We were told the story of Kunta Kinte's disappearance and how Alex Haley's detective work led him to Juffere.

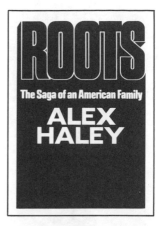

*"Roots"* was published in October 1976 and has sold millions of copies worldwide. It has been translated into thirty languages. An eight-part dramatization of *"Roots"* aired on television in 1977. This mini-series attracted one of the largest viewing audiences in television history.

One of the reasons Mr. Haley was successful in tracing his roots to The Gambia was because Kunta Kinte continued to use his African name even after he was enslaved and renamed Toby. The book *"Roots"* and the television series motivated many African Americans to name their children Kunta and Kizzie, after two of the main characters.

*The official griot of Juffere.*

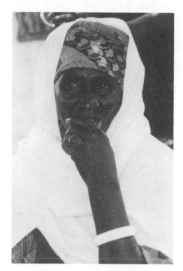

*Binta Kinte*

The people of Juffere were pleased to discover that Kunta Kinte was not killed after he was kidnapped. They were also pleased to see one of Kunta's *descendants* return home with the news, even though it did take almost 200 years. After our history lesson, the griot introduced us to an 83 year old woman named *Binta Kinte* (Ben TA KIN Tay) who was a distant cousin of both Kunta Kinte and Alex Haley.

We had an opportunity to talk with many of the children in Juffere before we boarded our bus and continued our drive to Banjul. When we arrived at our hotel we were assigned our rooms and later that evening we surprised my daddy with a birthday cake after dinner. Today was his 42nd birthday.

During the evening my father talked about how important it is to share birthdays with your family and friends. He asked us to imagine how we would feel if we were stolen away from our families and never saw home again. My father said, "We may not be able to find our African families like Alex Haley did; but we should never forget where our home is, and we should never forget those we left behind."

*The children of Juffere greeted us after their return from school.*

# Boat Ride on The Gambia River

The next morning, Tuesday, July 27, we prepared ourselves for an all day journey up The Gambia River to *James Island.* We traveled by motor boat for a distance of 15 miles (24 kilometers). It was a long and lazy ride as we snaked our way through the water. The Gambia River was so wide at one point that I could barely see the shore on either side. As we continued our journey the river became narrower and narrower.

*Granny and me sailing up The Gambia River.*

Riding up the river was almost like being lost in time. We didn't see any other people or buildings. Those on our boat relaxed by talking, singing songs and lying in the warm sun. The Gambians on our boat cooked fish that they had just caught and chicken which had been purchased from the market before we departed. We ate our meal on the boat as we sailed on the river.

After a couple of hours we reached James Island, which was named after King James of England. A fort was built on the island in the 17th-century in order to protect the British merchants who participated in the slave trade. This island was one of many on The Gambia River where the British gathered the Africans they stole before putting them on ships bound for the Caribbean or America.

Although most of the buildings at *Fort James* were destroyed, we could still see the rooms where the Africans were chained and beaten. We also saw numerous cannons that were used to defend the fort from other Europeans who wanted to steal the enslaved Africans from the British.

*Fort James was one of many forts and dungeons on The Gambia River which were used to enslave Africans.*

Who knows? James Island may have been the place where Kunta Kinte was taken after he was kidnapped from his village. If he had been stolen from the British, by the Portuguese or the French, he may have been taken to another part of the Americas, and Alex Haley would have never been born. This made me realize that there are millions of stories about millions of people which will never be told.

During our boat ride down The Gambia River back to *Banjul,* we had an opportunity to travel the same route as many of the enslaved Africans had years earlier. But we were much more fortunate. We were able to move about freely, eat lunch and enjoy ourselves. We knew where we were going, and that we would eventually go home.

## City Tour of Banjul

Wednesday, July 28, was our last day in The Gambia and we toured the city of Banjul, the capital. When The Gambia was ruled by the British the city was known as *Bathurst.* This city was founded in 1816 and was used as a base to seize the slave ships of other Europeans and to protect the ships of the British. In 1973, the city was renamed Banjul by the people of The Gambia.

Banjul is very small and it has a population of about 103,000. It is the largest city in The Gambia. Because of the country's small size there is very little land for farming and no valuable mineral resources. This is the major reason why The Gambia isn't as prosperous as Senegal.

Sir *Dawda Kairaba Jawara* (Da da Ka Ra Ba JaWor A) was the president of The Gambia and his face is on the paper currency. When we told the Gambians how good it was to see the face of an African on money, they couldn't believe that we didn't have any images of African Americans on our money.

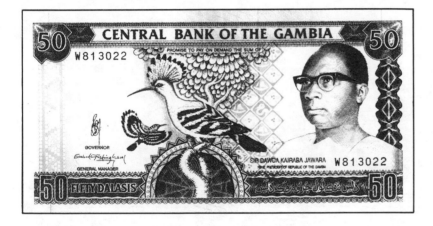

*The paper currency of The Gambia bears the image of its former president.*

Most of the people we met knew a lot about America by watching TV and the movies. They get *Black Entertainment Television (BET)* on cable and they watch all of the music videos. They really like our music and they know the names of most of our famous music stars, athletes and political leaders.

During our city tour we visited the National Museum and the market place. We also saw several craft shops where the women made beautiful tie-dyed clothing and wall hangings and the men made wonderful wood carvings.

# GHANA

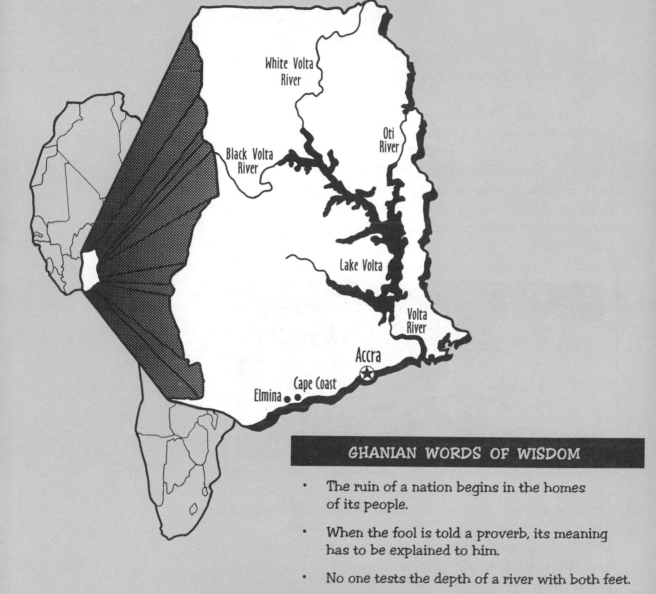

White Volta River

Oti River

Black Volta River

Lake Volta

Volta River

Accra

Cape Coast

Elmina

## Ghana

Official Name: Republic of Ghana
Area: 92,098 sq. mi. / 238,537 sq. km.
Population: 16,250,00
Capital City: Accra

Colonized By: England (1874-1957)
Name During Colonial Times: The Gold Coast
National Language(s): English; Twi, Fanti, Ewe,
National Religion(s): Traditional, Christian, Muslim

# Chapter 4

# Ghana

On Thursday, July 29, we said good-bye to Banjul and The Gambia and boarded a plane which would take us to our next destination, *Accra* (uh KRAH), the capital of Ghana. Our plane made one brief stop in *Conakry* (KAHN uh kree), the capital of *Guinea* (Gin ee) and then we were airborne again.

From the moment we landed in Ghana, everyone was very excited. Ghana is one of the most popular and productive countries in Africa. It has a rich history which dates back over 30,000 years. Some of the most important events in African history took place in this country.

Ghana has a population of over 16,250,000. It is slightly smaller than the state of Oregon and covers an area of 92,098 square miles (238,537 square kilometers). The *Ashanti* (Uh SHUN tee) make up the largest ethnic group in Ghana and the *Fanti* (Fan ti) group ranks second.

Even though English is the official language, many Ghanaians still speak their traditional languages of *Twi* (twee), *Fanti*, *Ewe* (E vay), and numerous others. Most of the people still practice their traditional religions. A large number are also Christians, and about 10 percent are Muslims.

Ghanaians had ruled their lands for thousands of years before they were invaded by the Arabs. But even under Arabic influences, the African traditions continued to flourish. When the Portuguese came to this area of West Africa in 1471, they discovered so much

*Kwame Nkrumah
(1909-1972)*

Nkrumah attended college at Lincoln University in Pennsylvania, where he shared ideas with many African Americans. After his return to Ghana, Nkrumah led his country in the struggle for independence from British colonialism in the 1950's. He served as Ghana's first president from 1960 to 1966. A memorial was built in his honor in the city of Accra.

gold, they called the region the "*Gold Coast.*"

Other European nations soon followed the Portuguese to Ghana when they realized it was a source of such great wealth. They fought each other for the gold until they realized they could make more money selling Africans as slaves. Between 1482 and 1877, Europeans either built or rebuilt about 60 forts and slave dungeons in Ghana. Today, about 20 remain and many are in a state of ruin.

In the late 1800's the Gold Coast became a colony of the British, which is why English is the official language. The Africans in the Gold Coast gained their independence from Britain in 1957, and they renamed the country "Ghana," the name of an ancient African kingdom.

*Dr. Kwame Nkrumah* (KWAH meh en KROO mah) became Ghana's first Prime Minister and he was elected president in 1960. Ghana is highly respected because it became the first African nation to free itself from European colonialism. Nkrumah inspired other Africans to become the rulers of their own countries and to fight against European colonialism.

As we drove from the airport through the city of Accra I saw skyscrapers, people, and cars everywhere. It was just like being at home during rush hour. When we arrived at our hotel we saw a number of very famous people while we were in the lobby waiting to check into our rooms. Most of them were African Americans who were in Ghana for several conferences and tours.

There were people attending conferences for the *National Association of Black Social Workers* and the *National Council for Black Studies.* Both of these organizations are based in the United States and held their conferences in Ghana because of its rich history.

# City Tour of Accra

The following morning, July 29, we prepared ourselves for an exciting tour of Accra, the political and administrative capital of Ghana. The city has a population of 1,200,000 and is located on the southern coast of Ghana, on the shores of the Atlantic Ocean.

During the morning we visited the *W.E.B. Du Bois* (do Boyz) Centre for Pan African Culture. Du Bois was a famous African American historian and sociologist. He was born in Massachusetts in 1868, and became the first African American to receive a Ph.D. from Harvard University.

Dr. Du Bois was a Pan-Africanist and he believed that all people of African descent had a common history and destiny. He moved to Ghana in 1961 after becoming dissatisfied with the treatment of Africans in America. Dr. Du Bois continued his studies and research until his death in 1963.

Du Bois was 95 when he passed away and his body is enshrined at the Centre. The Centre also houses a collection of his writings, numerous photographs and other memorabilia. The W.E.B. Du Bois Centre for Pan African Culture was created by the Ghanaians out of respect for the legacy of Dr. Du Bois. They wanted to make sure that his memory was never forgotten.

The Ghanaians built a similar memorial in honor of Dr. Kwame Nkrumah, the man who led Ghana to independence on March 6, 1957. Nkrumah is regarded by many as the "Father of modern Ghana." This part of the tour also reminded me of Washington, D.C. The major difference was that in Ghana all of the monuments, memorials and statues were built in honor of Africans.

*William Edward Burghardt Du Bois (1868-1963)*

Du Bois was one of the founding members of the NAACP. He was also one of the first advocates of Pan-Africanism. In 1900, Du Bois clearly defined the future of race relations in the United States when he declared that, "The problem of the twentieth century is the problem of the color line."

*Ghana commemorated its independence with the construction of this monumental arch located in the center of Accra.*

## ADINKRA SYMBOLS

**GYE NYAME**
(Except God)
Represents the
omnipotence and
immortality of God

**NKONSONKONSON**
(A chain)
Link which unifies the
living and the deceased -
Symbol for cooperation

**FINANKRA**
(The complete House)
Denotes safety or
security in a home

**OSRAM NE
NSOROMMA**
(Moon and star)
Love, faithfulness,
benevolence and femininity

*An artist explains the meaning of Adinkra cloth.*

Adinkra is a cloth which is stamped with various designs. The designs are carved into wood and laboriously applied by hand. There are hundreds of images which represent abstract symbols of proverbs, geometric shapes and stylized representations of animals, birds and flowers. Adinkra means "good-bye" and the cloth was originally worn at funerals to say good-bye to the departed. Today, Adinkra symbols are applied to a variety of cloths and other objects.

We also visited the Ghana National Theater which is a huge auditorium, as beautiful as any that I've seen at home. Most of the activities for the National Council for Black Studies conference were held there. The world famous Centre for National Culture and Art and Craft Bazaar is located nearby. It is a huge outdoor shopping mall and cultural center.

At the Art and Craft Bazaar we saw the *Kente* (KIN tay) and *Adinkra* (AH dink RA) cloth which are so popular among African Americans. We must have seen over 75 vendors selling all kinds of fabrics, clothing, hats and sandals. It was the most colorful mall that I had ever seen.

Beyond the clothing vendors was another area where dozens of artists sold wood carvings, masks, drums, metal jewelry, statues and other items. Practically everyone in our

*The University of Ghana at Legon*

**ADINKRA SYMBOLS**

**NKYINKYMIE**
Durability and devotion
to service in the face
of hardships

**MATE MASIE**
The retention of wisdom
and knowledge

**FUNTUMMIREKU
DENKYEMMIREKU**
(Two-headed crocodile
with one stomach)
Democracy and unity
within diversity

**AKOBEN**
(War horn)
A call to action for
defense or volunteerism

group boarded the bus with their arms full of items they had purchased. It was a great afternoon.

Before the day was over we visited the *University of Ghana* in the city of *Legon* (LAY gun). The University is located in the countryside on a large hill and is surrounded by trees. The campus is very modern and seems to spread out in all directions.

Most students live on campus and their classes run from October through June. We had an opportunity to visit the bookstore and several classrooms before returning to our hotel in Accra. This was, by far, our most exciting day, but it wasn't over yet.

After dinner some members of our group got together with members of another group and attended a program at a nearby hotel. The program featured presentations by *Dr. Na'im Akbar* (Na Eem  AK Bar), who was with our group and *Dr. Jawanza Kunjunfu* (JA Wonza KUN Ju Fu), who was with a group from Chicago. Everyone, from both groups, was talking about how exciting it was to be in Ghana and the wonderful friends they were making.

# Cape Coast and Elmina

On Saturday, July 31, we left Accra, by bus, for the Central Region of Ghana.  We were on our way to visit the infamous forts and slave dungeons of *Cape Coast* and *Elmina* (EL Me Na). As we drove west along the coast we saw miles and miles of beautiful beaches that were lined with tall palm trees.  On the other side of the road we passed a number of small fishing and farming villages.

It took us almost two hours to drive 75 miles (120 kilometers) to Cape Coast.  Cape Coast is a modern city with a population of 90,000.  It is the capital of the Central Region of Ghana. It has its own university, Cape Coast University, and a number of other interesting attractions. The history of the city is quite rich and also quite sad.

The town was originally called *Oguaa* (OH goo a), by the Fanti people who first lived there.  It was the site of a thriving market and the commercial center for the ancient Kingdom of Fetu in the 17th century.

The Portuguese were the first European settlers in Oguaa and they renamed it *Cabo Corso* (Ca BO  curso).  When the French arrived they called it *Cap Corso* and the English later renamed it "Cape Coast."  The English settled there in 1662 and they controlled the region for almost 300 years.  When the British ruled the Gold Coast they made Cape Coast the capital.

Unfortunately, Cape Coast is most well known for the huge fortress and dungeon which still stand there.  The fortress was originally built by the Swedes in 1653.  In 1660 it was captured by the British, who enlarged it in 1662.  The fort was captured by the Dutch in 1663 and then re-captured by the British in 1664.  The British expanded it again in 1673.

*Cape Coast Dungeon*

The fort was attacked by the French in 1703 and again in 1757. It was later rebuilt by the British who also constructed a number of smaller forts to protect themselves from other Europeans. The reason the Europeans were always fighting each other was because they wanted to control the land and have all of the gold and ivory for themselves.

Eventually the Europeans found it much more profitable to sell Africans than to mine gold or hunt elephants for their tusks. Many of the forts were converted to dungeons in order to house the Africans whom they stole while on raids or bought from other Africans.

Our visit to the dungeons at Cape Coast was similar to the one we made to Goree Island in Senegal. But the Cape Coast castle and dungeons were much larger. The cell where the young boys and men were kept was underground, very dark, and had tiny openings for air and light to enter. Sometimes 1,000 people were packed into this room which was designed to hold about 200. Every person was branded, on their back with a hot iron, to show that they were the property of the Europeans.

Branding irons were used to brand the enslavers' initials on the backs of the enslaved Africans.

*Enslaved African males
at Cape Coast dungeon*

The Africans who resisted this inhumane treatment and tried to escape were either killed or beaten and chained to the walls. Each cell had openings in the ceiling where food was thrown to the men below. These cells also had no bathroom facilities and we were told that the level of the floor had risen two feet because of the human waste that accumulated over a 200 year period. You can still see the scratches on the walls that were made by the people who struggled to climb out of the cells.

These inhumane and pitiful living conditions drove many of the men insane. Others died of various diseases, while some even starved to death. Almost every day, the bodies of those who died were thrown over the wall of the fort into the ocean below.

*Enslaved African females
at Cape Coast dungeon*

There was also a similar dungeon where young girls and women were imprisoned. It was smaller than the one for the men, and sometimes 500 females were crowded in a space that was designed to hold 150. They were subjected to the same treatment as the males. Many were often raped by the guards.

The imprisoned Africans were detained in the dungeons for one to two months before they were shipped abroad. When the slave ships from Europe arrived, the Africans were led from their cells through an underground passageway to the beach and then led aboard the waiting vessels.

By now it was becoming clear that the horrors of the slave trade were much worse than any of us ever imagined. We left Cape Coast dungeon

"On the slave ship, the quarters for the black women are always directly below the rooms of the officers and crew, separate from the black men. Sailors and officers are permitted to indulge their passion among them at their pleasure, and sometimes are guilty of brutal excesses that would disgrace human nature."
Dr. Alexander
Falconbridge, 1788

and went to a nearby restaurant for lunch. It was right by the shore and we were entertained by a group of young children who sang and danced while we ate. In the distance we could see our next destination, the slave dungeons of Elmina. It was hard to enjoy ourselves after seeing those sights.

*Youthful dancers entertained us as we lunched in Cape Coast.*

Elmina was originally a fort built by the Portuguese in 1482. It is believed to be one of the first structures made by Europeans in Africa. The Portuguese had come to this area looking for gold and they called the region "Elmina" which means, "the mine." In addition to gold, the Portuguese also made money by killing elephants and selling their ivory tusks in Europe.

In 1637, the Dutch stole the land from the Portuguese and enlarged the fort during their war with the British in 1666. By 1792, Elmina was converted from a warehouse of gold and ivory into a warehouse for human beings. Hundreds of thousands of Africans were imprisoned there and the Dutch built smaller forts to protect Elmina from the British. When the slave trade became unprofitable the Dutch returned to Europe and the British took control of Elmina in 1872.

The dungeons at Elmina were similar to the ones at Cape Coast. They also had dungeons for men, women and children. We were informed by our guide that the ground of both dungeons was considered sacred by the Africans who originally lived there. Recently, the Ghanaians have rebuilt new shrines in honor of those who suffered and died in the dungeons.

The dungeons at Cape Coast and Elmina were the point of departure for millions of Africans who made the Middle Passage across the Atlantic. Most of the Africans were taken to Brazil, which was colonized by the Portuguese. Large numbers were enslaved on plantations throughout the Caribbean by the French, Spanish, Dutch and British. Others were brought to North America and a smaller number were taken to Europe.

The journey across the Atlantic was a living nightmare for the Africans. They were packed into the slave ships like sardines in a can. Their ankles were chained together and many were forced to lie naked on the wooden planks of the ship. Nearly one fourth of the Africans died during the Middle Passage and their bodies were fed to the sharks who followed the slave ships from Africa to the Americas.

"Captain List was worse than his crew members in taking advantage of the defenseless female slave...Phillippe List pushed his brutality to the point of violating a little Negro girl of eight to ten years, whose mouth he closed to prevent her from screaming. He forced himself upon the girl for three nights and put her in a deathly state. This mistreatment and violence did so much damage to this Negro girl that she was sold in Saint Dominique for only 800 livres instead of the 1,800 livres she would have been worth."

Document from the Archives Departmentales Nantes, France, 1777

"If the Atlantic were to dry up, it would reveal a scattered pathway of human bones, African bones marking the various routes of the Middle Passage."
-Dr. John Henrik Clarke

Millions of Africans died during the Middle Passage. Some committed suicide, others died of various illnesses and many were murdered by the crew for the insurance.

One of the worse examples of this practice involved Captain Luke Collingwood of the British ship the *Zong*.

On September 6, 1781, Collingwood sailed from Africa to Jamaica with 440 enslaved Africans. By November 29, 66 Africans had died, many others were gravely ill.

Collingwood ordered 132 of the sickest Africans thrown overboard because his insurance covered death from drowning, not from illness. Collingwood filed a claim with his insurance company stating that the Africans had to be thrown overboard because of a shortage of available drinking water.

"Some of the slave captains were thieves and cheats working for absentee slave owners. They would load...350 slaves on a ship, list in their log 300, stop at a port and sell 50, and put the proceeds directly in their pocket."
-Dr. John Henrik Clarke

*The Africans who boarded the slave ships were never expected to see home again*

There is no official record of the number of people who died during the Middle Passage or those who lived, only to be sold in the "New World." We don't know the exact number of Africans who died in the slave dungeons or in the raids on the villages. Few records now exist because many were destroyed over the years.

It has been estimated that 50 million Africans survived the Middle Passage and about 13 million died. The slave trade lasted over 400 years. Even after the slave trade officially ended, Africans in North America, South America and the Caribbean had to wait dozens of years before they were eventually freed. The plantation owners delayed the news of freedom in order to get as much labor out of the Africans for as long as they could. There has never been a group of people treated like this in the entire history of the world.

*This 19th century photo depicts numerous African children aboard a slave ship.*

As we drove back to Accra, everyone was thinking about all they had seen and heard during the day. Very few of us were aware of this part of our history because we were never taught this information in school. People referred to this period in history as the *"African Slave Trade."* It should be correctly referred to as the *"European Slave Trade"* of Africans. The word *"Maafa"* (MA a FA) is another term that describes this human tragedy, it means "great disaster."

When we arrived at our hotel we had dinner and everyone began to prepare for our departure to the Ivory Coast the next morning. My father decided to stay in Accra for two more days so that he could attend the National Council for Black Studies conference. He planned to meet us in Abidjan on Tuesday for our return flight to New York.

# IVORY COAST

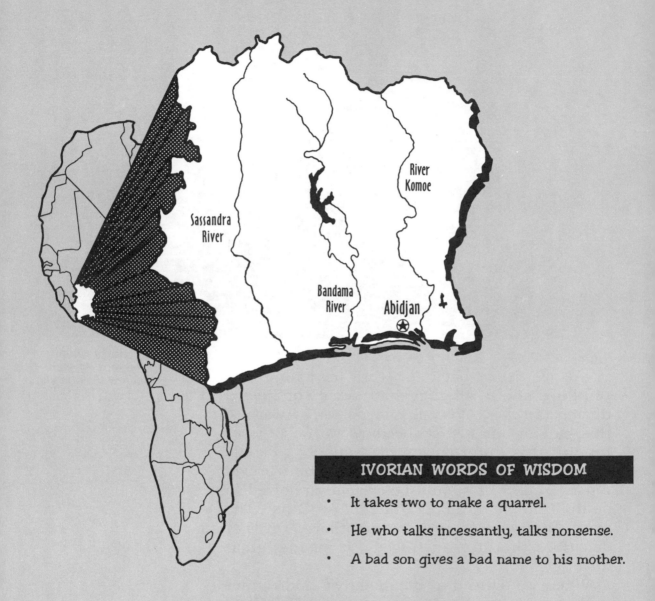

Sassandra
River

River
Komoe

Bandama
River

Abidjan

## IVORIAN WORDS OF WISDOM

- It takes two to make a quarrel.

- He who talks incessantly, talks nonsense.

- A bad son gives a bad name to his mother.

## Ivory Coast

__Official Name:__ Republique de Cote d'Ivoire
__Area:__ 124,500 sq. mi. / 322,500 sq. km.
__Population:__ 14,000,000
__Capital City:__ Abidjan

__Colonized By:__ France (1893-1960)
__Name During Colonial Times:__ Ivory Coast
__National Language(s):__ French; Malinke
__National Religion(s):__ Traditional, Muslim, Christian

# Chapter 5

# Ivory Coast

On Sunday, August 1, we left Ghana for the last part of our West African journey. We departed Accra for Cote d'Ivoire which is located on the western border of Ghana. Our plane landed a short time later in the coastal city of *Abidjan* (AB ih JAHN) which is the economic and administrative capital of Cote d'Ivoire.

Cote d'Ivoire is a French word which means "Ivory Coast" in English. Since none of us in the group spoke French, it was easier for us to pronounce the name of the country in English. Ivory Coast was colonized by the French and was once part of the European empire known as *French West Africa*. As you can probably guess, French is still the official language.

Ivory Coast was given its name by the French because of the fortune that was made by selling the ivory tusks of millions of slaughtered elephants. The French first arrived in the country in 1483 and they began enslaving the Africans about 1642. After the slave trade was abolished, Ivory Coast became a colony of France in 1893. On August 7, 1960, Ivory Coast declared itself an independent nation. Felix Houphouet-Boigny (Fe lix OO FWAY bwah NYEE), who led the independence movement, became the country's new president.

Ivory Coast has a population of about 14,000,000 and is 124,500 square miles (322,500 square kilometers) in size. It is slightly larger than the state of New Mexico, and has seven times the number of inhabitants. The countryside consists of thick rain forests and the coastal region has miles of beautiful beaches.

The people of Ivory Coast are from two basic groups, the Akhan and the Mandingo. There are more than 60 native languages spoken in the country and 60 per cent of the population practices traditional religions. Twenty-five per cent of the people practice Islam and fifteen per cent are Catholics.

After we arrived in Abidjan our group was transferred to our hotel. Many tourists refer to Abidjan as the "New York City of Africa." It has a population of 2,300,000 and all of the conveniences that one would expect to find in any major city in the U.S. Our stay in Ivory Coast was going to be a short one and tomorrow would be our only opportunity to do any sightseeing.

# City Tour of Abidjan

On Monday, August 2, we began our city tour with a drive through *Cocody (Ca CODY),* a residential district, which is an exclusive part of town that has a number of mansions and beautiful gardens. From there we continued down to the Adjame (AD jo MAY) Market where we saw vendors selling everything from food, to clothing, to carvings, masks and cooking utensils.

It was interesting to see how the old traditions have been mixed with the new ones. It seemed as though many of the people who had the better paying jobs, in government and business, were non-Africans. Many of them worked in the tall, air conditioned office buildings. On the other hand, the majority of

*City street in Abidjan.*

the Ivorians worked in small and crowded outdoor markets and earned much less money.

We also visited an area of Abidjan called *Treichville (TRYCH Vil)*, which our guide described as "a purely African district." It was obvious that this was the poor side of town. Treichville looked nothing like the neighborhood we saw earlier in the Cocody district. In some ways, the living and working conditions in the Ivory Coast reminded me of the poor neighborhoods back home.

Our tour also took us to the IFAN Museum, which has a collection of many artifacts depicting the history of the country. After leaving the museum we then drove to the *Banco* (BAN oh) *Forest* where we saw the famous *Banco Laundry men.*

The Banco Laundry men are mostly refugees who have settled in Ivory Coast and earn their living by doing laundry. There must have been hundreds of men in the river that morning washing clothes. It was an incredible sight watching the men wash clothing of every imaginable color, in the clear water against the background of blue sky and the green forest.

*The Banco Laundry men.*

The entire picture looked like a scene in a beautiful painting.

After the city tour, we returned to our hotel and prepared for our last night on the town. We were the guest of honor at a reception that was being hosted by some Marines from the U.S. who were stationed at the American Embassy in Abidjan.

Earlier in the year, one of the Marines had called my father to order some of his books. When my father told the soldier that we were coming to Abidjan, the soldier said that he, his friends and their families would love to meet us. They made arrangements for all of us to get together on our last evening in West Africa.

We were picked up at our hotel and driven to the Marine base where we were met by a group of military personnel and their families. They were all from different cities back home and were glad to meet some other African Americans. We had dinner and talked and took an awful lot of pictures. This was supposed to be a reception but it was more like a going away party. It was a great way to spend our last night in Abidjan.

# Chapter 6

# Return To New York City

Our group checked out of our hotel on Tuesday morning, August 3, and we were driven to the airport where we met my father, who had just arrived from Accra, Ghana. We all boarded a plane which flew us back to Dakar, Senegal. When we arrived in Senegal we had to spend about 14 hours at the airport because our flight to America was delayed. That long wait at the airport was definitely the most boring part of our trip.

Because of the long delay, we didn't arrive in New York until Thursday, August 5. Everyone was really glad to be back home because of our unexpected delay at the airport in Dakar. After we got our luggage we said good-bye to our friends. They went off to catch their various flights home and we loaded our belongings into our van for our trip home. Mr. Yusuf had returned to New York to pick us up for our drive back to Washington, D.C.

During the drive back home we reminisced about our trip and talked about all the places we saw, the people we met and the wonderful items that we brought back. The trip went by so fast it's hard to believe we had been gone for two weeks. But it was good to be back home and I was looking forward to sleeping in my own bed.

My father, grandmother and I say good-bye to Senegal.

While we were driving through the state of Maryland, we stopped to get some gas and something to eat. My father went to use the men's room and when he came back into the van he told us about an unsettling message that was written on the bathroom wall. The message said, "Death to all niggers - support the *KKK*."

My father said the people who wrote that message were no different from the people who built the slave dungeons we had seen in Senegal, The Gambia and Ghana. He said that there are still many people in the world who despise us simply because we are African. The illness which causes their hatred is still very much alive in America.

After we arrived home my father tried to explain some of these issues to me. He said that it was a very complicated situation, but that it was necessary for us to talk about it. My father believes that it is important I understand the history and nature of racist thought and behavior. He said that my future depends on it. Over the next weeks and months we had a number of conversations. We think it's important that we share some of those conversations with you.

Chapter 7

# Conversations
# With My Father

**Atlantis:**

Daddy, why did you get angry when you saw that message written on the bathroom wall about the KKK?

**Father:**

I get disturbed whenever I see signs of ignorance. The KKK and other European hate groups believe in the myth of "White Supremacy." They think that it is the destiny of whites, who represent less than 12% of the world's population, to dominate people of color and rule their land.

They believe that Africans are savages who are less than human. These people believe the lies they have written about Africans and they feel their hatred of them is justified. This hatred has been responsible for creating the behavior which has resulted in the murder of millions of Africans worldwide.

Over the centuries, scholars, scientists, politicians and priests have falsified the accomplishments of African people. They have said that Africans did not believe in God, they were cannibals and that they were incapable of any intellectual thought.

Lies are very powerful weapons. If a lie is told with conviction and repeated often enough, it will be accepted as a fact. For hundreds of

*As my father and I walked along the shore of Goree Island we talked about what we had learned from Mr. Ndiaye.*

The KKK (Ku Klux Klan) was formed by a group of Confederate Army veterans in Pulaski, Tennessee around 1866. Its members believed in the supremacy of whites and devoted themselves to neutralizing the freedoms of emancipated African Americans by engaging in terrorist activities.

Threats, murders, beatings, burnings, whippings and lynching were the methods most frequently used by the Klan. To hide their identities, Klan members wore pointed hoods and robes of white, draped sheets over their horses, and rode at night. Their membership grew rapidly in the Southern states of America and they became known as the Invisible Empire.

By 1924 Klan membership had peaked at 4.5 million and they were active in politics in the Southern, Northern, and Western states. Although Klan membership declined considerably by the 1950's there has been a resurgence in their activities since the 1980's. There are approximately 12,000 members of the Klan today.

years, scientists and theologians have said that Africans were inferior to Europeans. Africans were classified as sub-human in order to justify their enslavement and murder. Many racist groups such as the KKK perpetuate these myths as justification for their hatred of Africans in America.

Lies also have a profound affect upon the people who are being lied about. Enslaved Africans did not have access to information which would help them counteract the lies that were told about them. Many generations grew up believing these lies were true. As a result, many African Americans still believe in the truth of these lies and have developed deep feelings of insecurity and self-hatred.

*This cartoon, which appeared in a nationally syndicated magazine in 1874, openly endorsed racists views.*

**Atlantis:**

How can something that happened hundreds of years ago make people feel insecure today?

**Father:**

The reason people preserve their history and culture is so that they will have a record of their past accomplishments. This historical record instills a sense of awareness and confidence. It restores their identity, which is like a cultural memory that connects them to their past. It tells a people what they have done and what they are capable of achieving when they work together.

When knowledge is falsified or intentionally withheld from people, it effects their level of confidence. It is difficult for people to succeed in life if they lack confidence. Therefore, it is extremely important to encourage people to believe in themselves and their abilities.

When people are secure they are free from fear and danger. Fear leads to excessive anxiety which causes a person to act in a confused manner. When people are fearful, over anxious and confused, they will often be ill prepared to meet the challenges ahead of them. This behavior will cause a person to become unstable and unreliable.

When secure people come together, they strive to create secure communities where everyone can live with a greater sense of comfort. When insecure people come together, their communities are often filled with fear, sadness and pain. Lack of knowledge has a devastating effect on people and it often leads to abuse.

Black people who kill other black people, sell drugs to them and terrorize their neighbors, are expressing the ultimate acts of self hatred.

Between 1882 and 1946, there were 3,485 recorded lynchings of African Americans by white racists. In 1994 over 15,000 African Americans were murdered by other African Americans. Over half of those killed were youths, under the age of twenty, and an overwhelming majority were males.

There was a time when black communities were terrorized by whites in hoods, now they are being decimated by "Boys in the hood." In an effort to avert this crisis, many schools, churches and community organizations have begun to implement mentoring and rites of passage programs. Results have shown that youths who develop greater cultural awareness and self esteem are less prone to engage in violent activities.

People who are knowledgeable and secure create harmony in their communities. I believe that we can begin to correct some of the problems caused by self-hatred by teaching people to understand the effect their actions have on themselves and their community. History is one of the best ways to instill a greater sense of security and self worth in the minds of people.

**Atlantis:**

But most people think history is boring and it doesn't really seem that important.

**Father:**

Sometimes history is presented in a way which makes it appear boring, but it's much too important to be taken for granted. For example, your personal history began on the day of your birth. Much of the information vital to your being was recorded on your birth certificate. That is a part of your historical record.

Your name, address and telephone number are a part of your story too. They are facts which tell a person, who you are, where you live and how they can get in contact with you. Before you go to college, the institution will request a history of your academic record. Before you get a job, your potential employer will request a record of your performance and reliability. There is no aspect of life that doesn't involve history.

In church, you learn about the history of religion. In school, you learn about the history of civilization, language, math, science, art, music and so much more. You learn history from listening to the radio or watching television. You can't escape the influence of history. It takes on many shapes and forms, so you have to find a way to make it enjoyable.

**Atlantis:**

Do you mean that I have to find something about history that I like so that it won't seem boring?

**Father:**

Exactly. One of the reasons people think history is boring is because they don't know how to relate it to their personal lives. History is like a magical door which you can open in order to experience any event in the past. The information you gain from that experience can then be used to open doors to your future. Whatever you want to do in life has already been done by somebody else. If you study the lives of others, you will learn how to improve your own.

The reason I take you on trips to Africa is so that you can learn to apply the lessons from your ancestral history to your own life. That is exactly what you did when you returned from Egypt in 1989. You saw similarities between Egyptian symbols and symbols in the United States, and you wrote about them in your book.

**Atlantis:**

Yes, and many people told me that they were surprised to learn that the Washington Monument was a copy of the Egyptian tekhen, and that the pyramid and eye on the dollar bill were also African.

**Father:**

Do you realize that thousands of children and adults were introduced to African history when they read your book? Not only are you learning history, but you're in a position to write about history and teach it to others. When you write about your trip to West Africa people are going to learn from that experience too.

In April 1994, I traveled to Manchester, England with my father. While he did a presentation at the "Education of the Black Child, National Conference," I read passages from *My First Trip To Africa* to a group of children.

*Marcus Moziah Garvey
(1887-1940)*

Garvey was a Jamaican born African who is regarded as the leader of the "Black-to-Africa" movement. In 1914, he founded the Universal Negro Improvement Association (U.N.I.A.) which attracted millions of members who were known as "Garveyites." He moved to New York City in 1916 and continued to expand his organization.

Garvey stressed economic independence and raised over $10 million in two years. He used this money to establish restaurants, hotels and factories. In 1923, Garvey formed a shipping company called the Black Star Line. His goal was to provide transportation to return African Americans to Africa. Some of Garvey's ideas were looked upon unfavorably by the United States Government and he was deported to Jamaica in 1927. Many of Garvey's ideas continue to inspire Africans throughout the world.

When I was your age, I never learned much about Africa. I was profoundly influenced by television programs which usually portrayed Africa as a jungle, and Africans as savages. After college, I began reading books which gave me a different view of Africa, and when I finally traveled there, my eyes were opened to a whole new world. I want to open your eyes and have you experience Africa while you are young.

I want you to understand and appreciate the importance of your history and culture so that you can teach your children. If you teach your children well, they will pass their knowledge on to their children. I believe that it is the responsibility of all parents to teach children to appreciate their cultural and ancestral history.

*Marcus Garvey* said that, "A people without history is like a tree without roots." You can't see the roots of a tree, but without them the tree could not exist and it would not bear fruit. You are the fruit which was produced by your mother and me. We were produced by your grandparents and they were produced by your great grandparents who are now your ancestors. That history is recorded in our family tree.

### Atlantis:

I guess that's the reason Alex Haley called his book *"Roots."* He traced the branches of his family tree all the way back to their African roots. Do you think that we can ever do that?

### Father:

That may prove to be quite a difficult task to achieve. Your third cousin, Pauline, is the family historian and she has not been able to trace our family back more than three or four generations. She has been unable to find the birth records of our family members who left Alabama over fifty years ago. Unfortunately we are like millions of other Africans in America who will never be able to trace our family roots back to a specific African country.

This is exactly the reason why the Africans who were enslaved and brought to America were never allowed to teach their history or practice their culture. The European enslavers wanted to make sure that the children of the enslaved Africans would remain disconnected from their roots. Even our last names are the names of our former enslavers.

**Atlantis:**

That's so cruel. Why do people need slaves in the first place? It isn't right to take people away from their families and treat them so unfairly.

**Father:**

*Slavery* is as old as mankind. Throughout history, people have owned other people and forced them to work for them without any form of payment. The earliest slaves were usually prisoners of war or criminals. Slavery was once used as a form of punishment before jails were created.

The word *slave* is derived from the word *Slav* and was used to describe people of Slavic origin who lived in southeastern Europe. In ancient times the Greeks and Romans used slave labor to build their civilizations. During this period of history a slave was considered property and had no rights at all.

People have enslaved others in countries throughout Europe, Asia, and America. There have also been instances where people were enslaved because they worshipped a god who was different from the god of their enslavers.

Family reunions are important because they allow several generations of family members to get together and share their history. This logo above was designed by my father for our 1985 family reunion which was held in Chicago.

His grandfather's name was Eddie Walker and his grandmother's name was Mary Gunter. They were married in Alabama and later moved to Chicago.

The last names of my great-grandparents were derived from the last name of their grandparents who were enslaved in the south. Since our ancestors were given the last name of their slave masters, we will never know their real names or be able to trace our family roots back very far.

*Pope John Paul II at the "Door of no return."*

"Pope John Paul II passed through that door yesterday and toured the cells of the "house of slaves," begging forgiveness for the Christians involved in the slave trade...

'How can one forget the enormous suffering inflicted, ignoring the most elementary rights of man, on the people deported from the African continent?'

In remarks to the museum curator, John Paul referred to the 'drama of a civilization that called itself Christian.'

He called the house the 'tragic model' for the concentration camps...

Slavery is a theme the pope is expected to take up again when he visits the Dominican Republic in October to mark the 500th anniversary of the discovery of America and the arrival of Europeans in the New World."

The Associated Press
February 23, 1992

This happened frequently during the Crusades of the eleventh and twelfth centuries. The Christians enslaved the Muslims and the Muslims enslaved the Christians.

Africans have also enslaved other Africans. But there have been instances where they showed a little more respect for their slaves. Some were given the right to marry, have a family, and even own property. In some cases, slaves were even allowed to buy their own freedom. In these societies, a person may have been enslaved, but they were still considered human beings who had basic rights which were respected.

**Atlantis:**

If people all over the world have had slaves, then what makes the enslavement of Africans so different from others who were enslaved?

**Father:**

That's because Africans were subjected to the most brutal form of slavery humans have ever experienced. When the Portuguese went into Africa in 1441, they kidnapped Africans and sold them as slaves in Portugal. They called these people *Negroes* and considered them *pagans* because they were not Christians.

In 1442, Pope Eugenia IV gave the Portuguese permission to enslave all "pagan Negroes." By 1481, two other popes had given the kings of Spain and England permission to enslave Africans as well.

**Atlantis:**

I guess that explains why the pope went to Goree Island in 1992. I remember seeing a photograph of Pope John Paul II standing in the "Door of no return." Mr. Ndiaye told us that the pope had come there to ask God to forgive the Christians for enslaving African people. Maybe that's why Mr. Ndiaye had the picture in his office so that people would always remember why the pope had come to Goree.

**Father:**

That's exactly right. But another reason why the pope visited Goree in 1992 was to commemorate the 500 year anniversary of Columbus' arrival in the New World.

**Atlantis:**

What did that have to do with Goree Island?

**Father:**

After Columbus' voyages to the West in the 1490's, he returned home with foods that the Spanish had never tasted. When other Europeans finally experienced foods such as corn, tomatoes, tobacco, potatoes, sugar, coffee, and chocolate, they were very excited. These foods stimulated their taste buds and they had an appetite for more. European businessmen decided to establish plantations in the "New World" so that they could grow these foods and make a fortune selling them to the people back in Europe.

At first the Europeans enslaved the native people, whom they called *Indians,* and forced them to work on the plantations. Many of the Indians escaped and ran away into the hills.

The lands of North and South America were named after Amerigo Vespucci, an Italian-born explorer. Vespucci claimed to have sighted a vast continent (South America) in 1497, and believed that he had found a "New World." In 1507, a German map maker who believed that Amerigo was the first European to reach the New World suggested that it be named *America.*

Christopher Columbus, the Italian born explorer, had sailed to this same area in 1492. But Columbus mistakenly believed that he had sailed to lands off the coast of India. The term *Indians* was used by him to describe the original inhabitants of the lands that were later renamed by Europeans.

*European explorers in the "New World."*

Thousands of others died of the diseases which the Europeans brought with them to the "New World." Without the labor to harvest the crops, most of the food rotted in the fields.

In order to solve this problem, Europeans decided that they would enslave Africans and sell them to the European plantation owners in America. The Africans were considered to be much stronger than the Indians and they could work harder and longer hours. By importing Africans to America, it would be difficult for them to run away since they didn't know the land and were thousands of miles from home. They were also easier to identify.

Between 1451 and 1870, Europeans made billions of dollars from the sale of Africans. Cities like Liverpool, England; Seville, Spain and Nantes, France became the capitals of the European Slave Trade. Thousands of people invested their life savings in the factories that were created to make the chains and build the ships which would be used to shackle and transport enslaved Africans.

## EUROPEAN NATIONS INVOLVED IN THE ENSLAVEMENT OF AFRICANS

|  | Beginning of Involvement | End of Involvement |
|---|---|---|
| PORTUGAL | 1444 | 1870 |
| SPAIN | 1479 | 1835 |
| ENGLAND | 1562 | 1807 |
| UNITED STATES | 1619 | 1861 |
| HOLLAND | 1625 | 1803 |
| FRANCE | 1642 | 1860 |
| SWEDEN | 1647 | 1825 |
| DENMARK | 1697 | 1792 |

While the ships were being built in Europe, money was also being invested to build the slave dungeons in Africa. Men were hired to buy Africans and detain them in the dungeons until the ships arrived. Back in Europe, crews were hired to man the ships and captains were hired to command them. Insurance companies were also established to insure that investors would not loose their money if something were to happen to the ships during the long and dangerous voyage.

After the ships were built, they sailed from Europe to West Africa where the captains purchased the Africans who were held captive in the slave dungeons. The ships were loaded to capacity and then sailed across the Atlantic to America. The Africans who survived the Middle Passage were sold to the European plantation owners in South America, the Caribbean and North America.

A United Nations' sponsored study stated, "In the (ten) years between 1783 and 1793 Liverpool, England put 878 ships into trade (and) shipped 303,737 Negroes from Africa." This business transaction netted over 15 million pounds within a ten year period.

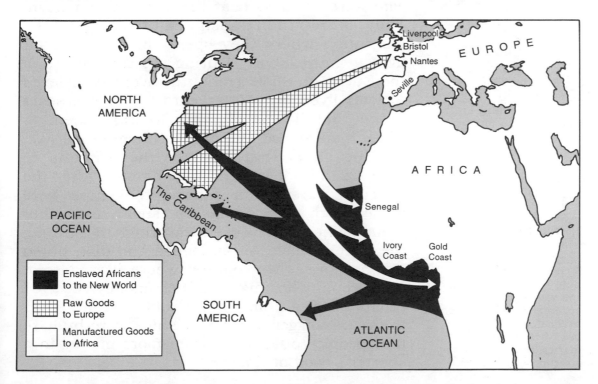

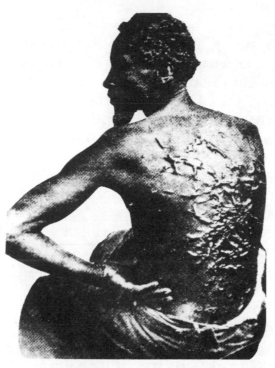

*Enslaved Africans were often brutalized by their overseers. This man's back bears the scars of numerous beatings.*

The European Slave Trade produced tremendous wealth for many European nations. Various industries were developed which later led to the establishment of numerous "legitimate enterprises." In England, the city of Birmingham was famous for the iron mills which forged the chains used to enslave Africans. The city of Liverpool was one of the primary sites where slave ships were built. The insurance policies which were issued to the slave ships were frequently underwritten by financial institutions in London.

The Africans were *"seasoned"* by overseers who were hired to beat them into submission. They were then assigned tasks on the plantation where they spent the rest of their lives at hard labor. During the early years of the European Slave Trade, the average enslaved African lived only five years. The overseers found that it was cheaper to work them to death than to feed and care for them properly.

The ships that brought the Africans to America did not return home empty. After the Africans were taken ashore, the ships were loaded with rum, molasses, sugar and other items. When the vessels returned to Europe, the merchandise was unloaded and distributed to warehouses and stores where it was sold. The people who invested their money received profits ranging from 400 to 1,000 percent. Over the years, bigger and faster ships were built so that people could make even more money in a shorter period of time.

The enslavement of Africans was nothing more than a business to the Europeans. It was a business which prospered for over 400 years. The Africans who were enslaved were responsible for developing the wealth of Europe and America. And the poverty that you see in Africa today is a by product of slavery and colonization.

The enslaved Africans possessed many skills. They were carpenters, blacksmiths, stone masons, farmers, tailors, cooks, healers and educators. These collective talents were used to build the farms, plantations and towns in the West. The people who owned the Africans became increasingly wealthy while those who did the actual labor received little or no benefits.

If this horrible event had not occurred, the world would be much different than it is today. America and Europe would not be as wealthy and Africa would not be as poor. You have to

Enslaved African Americans worked from sunup to sundown, 12 to 18 hours a day, depending on the season. They toiled on the plantations for six days a week and were only allowed to rest on Sunday's. Over 12 generations of African Americans worked without receiving adequate payment for their labor.

Slavery in the United States lasted from 1619 until 1865. During that period, African labor was responsible for:
- Clearing millions of acres of land for farms and factories
- Supplying enough wood to build thousands of homes and hundreds towns
- Harvesting the crops which supplied food and clothing for millions of people in Europe and the Americas.

If African Americans had been fairly compensated for their labor, their decedents would now be the owners of numerous businesses and enterprises. Many African Americans are currently seeking reparations for the labor of their ancestors.

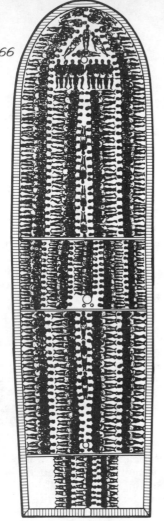

*Floorplan of a 'tight pack' slave ship.*

"...a question arose between the slave sellers and shippers over 'tight pack' versus 'loose pack.' If they packed the slaves tight...large numbers would die...one-third to one-half wouldn't reach the market. But if they packed them loose, they'd have enough breathing space that a goodly number of them would live through the ordeal and get to the market. So, the argument became: 'is it more economical to loose pack or tight pack?' No one was talking about or thinking about the Africans as human beings."
-Dr. John Henrik Clarke

understand that practically every black person you see in North America, South America, Central America and the Caribbean Islands, is descended from Africans who were brought to these lands hundreds of years ago.

## Atlantis:

Do you mean that all the black people in Chicago, Washington, D.C., New York are related to people who were stolen from Africa?

## Father:

Yes, that's right. Africans didn't come to America seeking freedom, like the European immigrants. Africans were brought to the "New World" as a source of free slave labor. They worked for European immigrants who made a fortune in a land which was stolen from the original inhabitants.

The enslavement of the Africans was the largest forced migration in world history. It is estimated that over 50 million people survived the Middle Passage and were enslaved in the New World. About 2.5 million Africans were brought to North America and the 30 million African Americans living today are their descendants.

## Atlantis:

What happened to the rest of the Africans who were brought over to America?

## Father:

Approximately 20 million Africans were taken to *Brazil* which was colonized by the Portuguese around 1500. Another 20 million were taken to a dozen Caribbean Islands where they were colonized by the British, French, Spanish and Portuguese. Five million Africans were scattered throughout Mexico and South

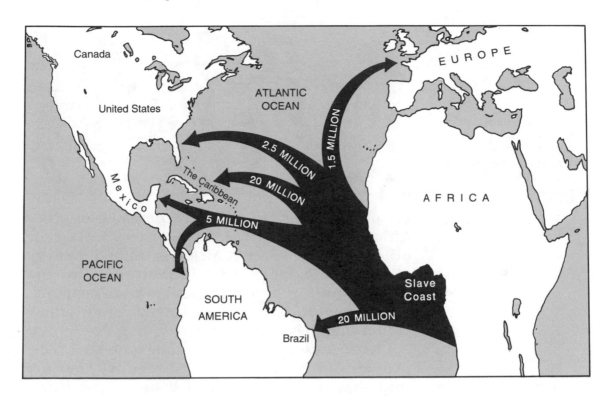

America by the Spanish, and about 1.5 million were taken to Europe.

Today, Brazil has a population of over 103 million people of African descent. It has the largest concentration of Africans living outside the continent of Africa. African descendants are the primary inhabitants of the Caribbean Islands and there are large numbers of Africans living throughout Mexico, Central and South America.

This map illustrates the flow of enslaved Africans into the Americas and Europe. Although the actual number of Africans who survived the Middle Passage is unknown, we have used a conservative figure of 50 million to represent the Maafa. Estimates of the numbers of Africans enslaved and killed during the European Slave Trade range form a low of 11.5 million to highs in excess of 100 million.

## Atlantis:

How were the Europeans able to enslave so many Africans? Didn't they try to fight back and defend themselves?

## Father:

In the early days of the European Slave Trade, many Africans sold their own people to the Europeans. At first they sold their

The Africans captured in village raids were restrained by numerous devices and forced to walk dozens of miles to the slave dungeons on the coast.

prisoners of war but when the demand for other Africans increased, the slave traders looked for other sources. Some Africans raided nearby villages and sold the inhabitants to the Europeans for money, jewelry and weapons. These people willingly betrayed their fellow countrymen because of greed.

I have read that some Africans who sold their people into bondage had no idea of the fate that awaited them. They foolishly believed that the enslaved Africans would be treated with some degree of humanity. But during the European Slave Trade, all Africans were regarded as less than human and they had no rights which were respected. Even the African slave traders were sold into slavery if the Europeans felt they weren't supplying them with enough people.

The enslaved Africans often didn't always have guns, rifles or cannons with which to defend themselves, but they fought back as best they could. There are numerous stories of Africans who successfully defended their homelands against foreign invaders. In Ghana, Queen Mother *Nana Yaa Asantewa* (NaNa Ya A Santa Wa) led the Ashanti Nation in a bitter war against the British. After an intense year-long battle she was captured and sent into exile, but her people continued to struggle against their oppressors.

*Nana Yaa Asantewa*

Yaa Asantewa was the Queen Mother of the Ejisu district in the Gold Coast. She led the Ashanti nation in its struggle against British colonialism in 1900.

*The 53 Africans on board the slave ship Amistad staged a successful rebellion in July 1839.*

There were also instances where Africans liberated themselves from their captors. In 1839, an African named *Cinque* (Sin Que) led a mutiny aboard the *Amistad* (Ami STAD), a slave ship which was bound for a port in Cuba. Cinque and his 52 followers killed the captain of the ship and forced the surviving crewmen to sail back to Africa. The crewmen tricked Cinque by sailing East during the day and then sailing Northwest during the night. After two months at sea the Amistad arrived in New York where Cinque and his followers were arrested by U.S. Naval authorities.

All of the Africans aboard the Amistad were charged with murder and mutiny and they endured an 18-month trial in New London, Connecticut. Their case went all the way to the Supreme Court and the Africans were eventually freed in February 1841. Cinque and 34 surviving members of the Amistad takeover left Connecticut and returned to their home in *Sierra Leone* (sih AIR uh lee OHN) in 1842.

There were many Africans who did not submit to enslavement. They fought at home and they fought on the slave ships, and they continued to fight their captors even after they arrived in America.

*Cinque*

*Harriett Tubman
(1820?-1913)*

Harriet Tubman was an enslaved African who was born in the state of Maryland. She made her escape from slavery in 1849 and became one of the most famous conductors on the *Underground Railroad.* In 1857, Tubman led her parents to freedom and she never lost a passenger on any of her 19 rescue missions.

Tubman also served as a nurse, scout and spy for the Union Army during the Civil War (1861-1865). During the war she also was responsible for helping to free 750 Africans. Harriet Tubman continued to work for the betterment of African people throughout her long life.

**Atlantis:**

I remember you telling me about *Harriet Tubman.* She escaped from slavery and returned to the South 19 times to help over 300 Africans escape to freedom in the North.

**Father:**

That was her way of fighting the enslavers.

**Atlantis:**

When I was younger you used to read me a poem about Harriet Tubman. The poem was in a book entitled *"Honey I Love,"* which was written by *Eloise Greenfield.* You took me to meet her in 1988, and she autographed my book.

**Father:**

You've got a pretty good memory. I believe you were just five years old when I used to read that poem to you.

**Atlantis:**

Were there many other people like Harriet Tubman who helped Africans escape from the South?

**Father:**

Yes. There were over 3,000 people who served as guides on the *Underground Railroad.* Of course, it wasn't a real railroad. This term describes the secret trails that Africans followed as they escaped on foot. Those who led them along the trails were called "conductors." The groups would travel by night and rest during the day at homes that were designated as safe houses.

Many of the safe houses had secret rooms and passageways where the Africans could hide from those in pursuit of them. After a hearty meal and several hours rest, the Africans would wait until darkness and continue their journey to freedom in the North. The

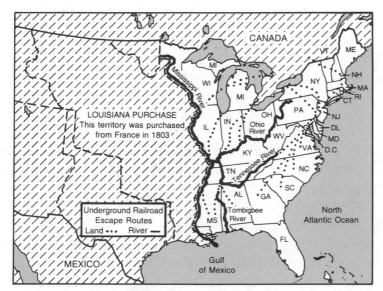

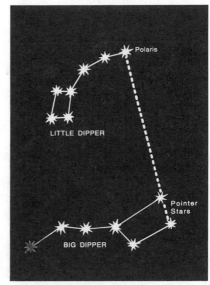

*The Drinking Gourd*

conductors would lead their groups through streams, rivers and swamps in an effort to keep the bloodhounds from picking up their scent and catching them. It was an extremely dangerous job.

Africans navigated through the darkness by following a group of stars which they called the *Drinking Gourd*. A gourd is a plant which is shaped like a dipper and was used to drink water. The *Drinking Gourd* is a constellation which we call the Big Dipper and it points to *Polaris* (Po lar is), the *North star*. By following the North star, over 75,000 Africans were able to find their way to freedom in the Northern states of America and in Canada.

There were other Africans such as *Nat Turner* and *Gabriel Prosser (GA bri el PROS SIR)* who planned major rebellions in the state of Virginia in the early 1800's. Africans in America were inspired by the Africans in the Caribbean who led many successful revolts against their European enslavers. These African freedom fighters were called *Maroons (Ma runes)*, which is a Spanish term that refers to runaway cattle, horses and men.

The *Drinking Gourd* is better known as the constellation called the *Big Dipper*. The two stars at the front of the dipper point to *Polaris*, the *North Star*. Polaris is the last of a series of stars which form the handle of the Little Dipper.

Harriet Tubman was able to find her way North without the aid of a compass by drawing an imaginary line from the Pointer Stars in the Big Dipper to the North Star. Young children on the plantations were taught a song entitled "Follow The Drinking Gourd" which taught them the meaning of Polaris, how to find it, and how to follow it to freedom.

*Statue of Yanga, in the state of Veracruz.*

In Mexico, an enslaved African named *Yanga* led a group of Maroons in a war of liberation against the Spanish. Yanga and his followers defeated their former captors and established a free settlement in the mountains of Mexico around 1612. Yanga became the first governor of the town which was also named in honor of him. An annual festival is held in August to honor the memory of the former Congolese Prince who led his people to freedom.

The Maroons in Jamaica fought the British in a war of liberation which lasted for 140 years. One of their greatest military leaders was an African named *Cudjoe*. By 1730, Cudjoe and his army had terrorized the English settlers so badly that they strongly considered returning to England. Ultimately, the governor of Jamaica signed a peace treaty with Cudjoe giving him a large parcel of land and permission to hunt anywhere on the island, except within three miles of a European settlement.

Cudjoe and his Maroon followers accepted the terms of the agreement and lived the rest of their lives in freedom. Today, over 200 years later, there is still a thriving Maroon community living in the mountains of Jamaica. What's important to remember is that only those who fought for freedom achieved it. The Africans who did not join the Maroons remained enslaved until 1808, when slavery was abolished in Jamaica.

On the Caribbean island of *Saint Dominique*, between 1791 and 1802, an African named *Toussaint L'Ouverture* (Too SAN loo vehr TOOR) engaged the French colonists in a heated war of liberation. Toussaint was regarded as a brilliant military leader who won numerous battles against the French and forced them to flee the island. Toussaint L'Ouverture became the governor of the republic which was renamed *Haiti*.

The French continued their efforts to regain control of Saint Dominique because it was the richest of the French colonies and had an annual export trade of two and a half billion gold francs. The loss of this territory created financial difficulties for France which was also facing the possibility of war with Great Britain.

*Toussaint L'Ouverture (1743-1803)*

In 1803, *Napoleon Bonaparte*, the ruler of France, agreed to sell the Louisiana Territory to the United States for fifteen million dollars. This transaction was called *The Louisiana Purchase* and it added 827,987 square miles (2,144,476 square kilometers) to the western boundary of the United States, nearly doubling the size of the country.

Fifteen states were later formed out of this newly acquired region. I think it's safe to say that if Toussaint L'Ouverture had not challenged Napoleon's power in Haiti, France might have held on to the Louisiana territory a bit longer.

Although he was born into a life of enslavement, Toussaint rose to become the leader of a revolt on the island of Saint Dominique. Although he was later captured and imprisoned in France, he was admired by both his fellow countrymen and the French.

Some French writers considered Toussaint to have military and administrative skills which surpassed those of Napoleon. He was described by one French writer as, "The Black Napoleon-whom the White Napoleon imitated and killed."

## THE END OF AFRICAN ENSLAVEMENT IN THE WEST

| Year | Country | Year | Country |
|------|---------|------|---------|
| 1803 | HAITI | 1853 | ARGENTINA |
| 1808 | JAMAICA | 1863 | UNITED STATES |
| 1814 | GUYANA | 1870 | PANAMA |
| 1814 | TRINIDAD | 1870 | VENEZUELA |
| 1815 | MARTINIQUE | 1870 | SPANISH COLONIES |
| 1815 | GUADELOUPE | 1870 | PERU |
| 1815 | FRENCH COLONIES | 1873 | PUERTO RICO |
| 1823 | CHILE | 1886 | CUBA |
| 1830's | MEXICO | 1888 | BRAZIL |

*Nat Turner
(1800-1831)*

Nat Turner was born into a life of enslavement on a plantation in Virginia. Turner's father was born in Africa. He was captured and brought to America but later escaped and somehow managed to returned to Africa. Nat Turner attempted to escape too. He was caught and severely beaten.

Turner was also a dynamic preacher who said that God wanted him to liberate enslaved Africans. On September 1, 1831, Turner and his followers initiated the most famous slave revolt in United States history.

Before his capture, Turner and his men managed to kill over 60 whites in Virginia. Fear spread throughout the state and an army of over 800 marines and militia was engaged to hunt Turner down. During his trial, Turner maintained his right to obtain freedom for Africans at any cost. He was hanged on November 11, 1831.

The bravery of men such as Toussaint, Cudjoe and Yanga inspired thousands of Africans, who were enslaved in the United States to fight for their freedom. The actions of Gabriel Prosser, Nat Turner and Harriet Tubman sent shock waves of fear throughout plantations in the South. European Americans began to realize that as long as Africans were enslaved in the Americas, there would be no peace.

## Atlantis:

I never knew that so many Africans fought for their freedom. We always see pictures of them singing and dancing in the fields but I've never heard about how brave they were.

## Father:

There is a vast history about slavery which we have never been taught. Until recently, we seldom read about African freedom fighters in books or saw their stories in movies. There exists in this society an unwritten law which says that it is all right to show Africans as slaves, singing and dancing. But it is not all right to show them fighting to overcome the system which enslaved them.

As a result of this one-sided view of history, many of our people are too embarrassed by slavery to discuss it openly. Realistically, the people who should be embarrassed by slavery should be those who profited from it. People seldom question the lack of spirit and humanity that was shown by those who developed the institutions which benefited from the enslavement of African people.

If more African Americans were aware of the countless souls who struggled to achieve their freedom, they would view that period of history quite differently. This act of awareness brings to mind the term, *Sankofa* (SAN KOE FA), which means, "One must go back and reclaim the past in order to prepare for the future." It is a saying which comes from the Akan people of Ghana.

**Atlantis:**

We went to see a movie called *"Sankofa"* a few months ago.

**Father:**

Yes, we did. Do you remember what the film was about?

**Atlantis:**

*"Sankofa"* was about an African American model named Mona who visited Cape Coast Dungeon with her photographer. She had no knowledge of her history and was sent back in time so that she could experience life as a slave. When Mona finally returned to the present she was a changed woman. She had developed a greater understanding and appreciation of her African identity.

**Father:**

That was a good overview of the film. *"Sankofa"* was written, produced and directed by *Haile Gerima* (HY lee GE ree Ma), an African filmmaker who teaches at Howard University. *"Sankofa"* has won many international awards but movie distributors in America have refused to handle the film. They claimed that the film would not make any money because it was "too black!" Movie distributors would rather show films of black people selling drugs and killing each other than show a film which teaches black people to be proud of their African heritage.

Music, television and film have been found to influence the thinking and behavior of people, especially the youth. If you see negative

*Haile Gerima*
*(Independent Filmaker)*

"Film is used to interpret our reality, to do something about our condition, to activate people; to even make people rise up against a system that is racist and make it change."
Haile Gerima

Sankofa is an *Akan* word which means, "return to the past in order to go forward." The feet represent forward movement. The neck reaches back and has within its mouth an egg which represents the future.

*The Sankofa Bird*

In 1992, Bill Cosby accused the television networks of generating programs which constantly portray African Americans in a comical and negative light. He referred to these portrayals as "drive-by-images" which help to create and perpetuate negative stereotypes.

images and hear derogatory language often enough, you will grow to accept it as normal. It is not normal, nor is it healthy, for black people to consistently put each other down. This is one example of learned negative behavior.

I often hear young people use the word "nigger" or "niggas" when referring to their friends or themselves. Many of them believe that it is a term of endearment. That term "nigger" was created by Europeans and refers to an African who has no value. There is no such thing as a "nigger" and that word should not be a part of our vocabulary.

When I was younger, boys would often play a game called "the dozens." The objective was to talk so badly about a person that you would embarrass them and make them cry. One of the worse things that you could do was to talk about someone's mother and call her derogatory names; this would always lead to a fight.

When I was older I learned that "playing the dozens" was an activity that was carried over from the days of enslavement. In those times, all Africans who were old and crippled were sold in groups of twelve. Thus, "the dozens" referred to a group of Africans who were considered worthless and not as good as the healthy ones.

Today, they call "the dozens," "jonin'" or "snappin'," but the objective is still the same - the total humiliation of another human being. Most of the programs on television, such as *The Fresh Prince of Bel Air* and *Martin*, feature black people who frequently put each other down.

That type of behavior is a direct carry over from the days of enslavement. It wasn't funny then and it isn't funny now. You will also notice that practically every television program with an African American cast is a comedy. You will seldom see shows which portray black people in a serious manner. This suggests that we are incapable of acting intelligently or being taken seriously.

If books, television, radio and film are not going to give you positive images and desirable role models, then you must create them yourself. That is exactly what Africans did when they were enslaved. They created stories about various animals which taught their children how to cope with the pressures of enslavement.

Many of these stories featured small and clever characters who used their brains to outsmart a larger and more powerful enemy. One such character was known to the Akan of Ghana as *"Anansi* (a NUN See) *the Spider."* He became known as a female named *"Aunt Nancy"* to African Americans. The Hare, in African folk tales became known as *"Brer Rabbit"* in the United States and his chief enemy was known as *"Brer Fox."*

These characters were metaphors for human beings. "Brer Rabbit" represented the enslaved African and "Brer Fox" was the European overseer. The rabbit always outsmarted the fox and was able to keep from being caught and destroyed. When European Americans began telling these stories, "Brer Rabbit" became "Bugs Bunny."

**Atlantis:**

Are you saying that the Bugs Bunny cartoon came from fables that were invented by Africans who came to America?

**Father:**

Sure. Animated cartoons were created to teach children about life while they were being

"Do you think that (TV executives and audiences) will accept a black (character) who can outwit the smartest white guy, or who is powerful because he has the might of government behind him? The mindset (among program creators) is, 'People aren't going to believe that a black man is so powerful that he can pick up the phone and call the governor.' So they make the black character one-dimensional or a sidekick or a comedian."

Robert Johnson
President of BET
(Black Entertainment
Television)

*Brer Rabbit*

*Aesop
(c. 560 B.C.E.)*

"The influence of Aesop on Western thought and morals is profound. Plato, Socrates, Aristophanes, Aristotle, Solon, Cicero, Julius Caesar, Caxton, Shakespeare, La Fontaine, and the other great thinkers found inspiration in his words of wisdom.

The books that have been written about him and his works would fill an immense library. His writings have been translated into almost every language in the civilized world."

J.A. Rogers,
*World's Great Men of Color, volume I*

entertained. The relationship between characters such as Tom and Jerry, the Roadrunner and the Coyote, Tweetie Bird and Sylvester the Cat are cartoon stereotypes which parallel African fables. Modern cartoons illustrate how a big and powerful character can be easily defeated by a smaller character who uses his or her brains.

As a child in elementary school, I was fond of reading *Aesop's Fables*. Each character possessed human qualities and every fable taught a moral lesson. Years later, when I entered high school, I discovered that *Aesop* (EE Sahp) was an African who had been enslaved in Greece around 560 B.C.E. In fact, the name Aesop was derived from the Greek word "Ethiop," which means "burnt face" or "black."

African and African American educators were responsible for creating numerous ideals that have profoundly influenced the world. Our ancestors were creative musicians who invented soul music, jazz, spirituals, reggae and rap. They were also brilliant scientists and engineers who developed numerous devices that have made life easier for millions of people.

When you consider the pain and suffering that Africans have endured throughout generations of enslavement, segregation, and racism, it's a miracle that we are alive today. That miracle is proof of the indomitable spirit of African people. It is a spirit that lives within each of us. It is the spirit of Sankofa.

Sankofa is the process of returning to your roots in order to gather the wisdom necessary to lead a meaningful life. As you mature you will realize that life is like a test, the more you review your lessons, the better you will do on the final exam.

I take you to Africa so that you can study your past, take pride in your heritage, and become an active participant in determining the future of African people. This knowledge will help you survive in a competitive world that is sometimes unfair.

It is your responsibility to learn these lessons and teach them to your children, so that they will pass them on to their children. Always remember that I love you, I believe in you, and I know that you will make your family and your ancestors proud.

**Atlantis:**
Thank you Daddy, and I love you too!

# Glossary

Abidjan: (AB ih JAHN) The capital city of Ivory Coast.

Accra: (uh KRAH) The capital city of Ghana.

Adinkra: (AH dink RA)  A Ghanaian cloth which is hand printed with
   various symbols.  These Adrinka symbols represent numerous themes,
   proverbs and objects.

Adjame: (AD jo MAY) A famous market in Abidjan, Ivory Coast.

Aesop: (EE sahp) An African enslaved in Greece, around 500 B.C.E.  He was
   famous for his wit, intelligence and storytelling abilities.

Aesop's Fables: Works of Aesop which featured animals or insects as the
   main characters.  Each fable taught a moral lesson.

African Slave Trade: (See *European Slave Trade*)

Akbar, Dr. Na'im: (AK Bar) Prominent African American psychologist and
   author.

Amistad: (Ami STAD) A slave ship which was commandeered by enslaved
   Africans in Cuba in 1839.

Ancestors: Deceased persons from whom you are descended.  An ancestor
   can be a member of your immediate family or historical family.

Anansi the Spider: (a NUN see) A mischievous character in West African
   fables who became known as "Aunt Nancy" in the fables of African
   Americans.

Apartheid: (ah PAHRT tate) A racist system of segregation which was
   enacted by law in South Africa.

Asantewa, Nana Yaa: (NaNa Ya A Santa Wa) Queen Mother of the Ashanti in
   Ghana.  She led the Ashanti Nation in a war of liberation against the
   British Colonists during the early 20th century.

Ashanti: (uh SHUN tee) One of the major ethnic groups of ancient and modern Ghana.

Banco Forest: (BAN oh) A vast enclave of virgin forest in Ivory Coast.

Banco Laundry men: Refugees from across West Africa who work in Ivory Coast as laundry men. Their work is performed in the waters which flow through the Banco Forest.

Banjul: (BAN jul) The capital city of The Gambia.

Baobab Tree: (BAY oh bab) A tree which grows in the savannas of West Africa. It has a thick trunk and short branches with sparse leaves. The baobabs are used in numerous rituals in West Africa.

Bathurst: City ruled by the British during the colonization of The Gambia. It was renamed Banjul in 1973.

Big Dipper: A dipper-shaped group of stars in the constellation of Ursa Major. This group of stars helped enslaved Africans find their way north as they traveled along the Underground Railroad.

Black Entertainment Television: (BET) An African American owned cable television network.

Bonaparte, Napoleon: (BON' uh part, NA' POL eon) A former general who ruled France as emperor from 1804 to 1814.

Brazil: A South American country colonized by the Portuguese in 1500. Brazil is currently home to 103 million people of African descent.

Brer Fox: (Brother) A mythical character in African American folklore who symbolized the European overseer.

Brer Rabbit: (Brother) A mythical character in African American folklore who personified the enslaved Africans and represented their ability to survive by their wits.

Burroughs, Dr. Margaret: Educator & Artist. Co-founder of the DuSable Museum of African American History in Chicago, IL.

Bush: The grasslands of Africa. (See *Savanna*)

Cabo Corso: (Ca BO curso) Portuguese name for the ancient city of Oguaa in the central region of Ghana. (See *Oguaa*)

Cape Coast: Formerly Cabo Corso, a city in the central region of Ghana which was renamed by the British in 1662. (See *Oguaa*)

Cape Coast Dungeon: A huge slave dungeon and fortress in Ghana, originally built by the Swedes in 1653. It was later rebuilt by the French and British.

Cinque: (Sin que) An enslaved Congolese prince from Sierra Leone who led a successful rebellion aboard the slave ship *Amistad*.

Clarke, Dr. John Henrik: The distinquished African American elder, historian and professor emeritus at Hunter College in New York City.

Cocody: (Ca CODY) An exclusive residential district in Abidjan, Ivory Coast.

Colonization: The establishment of settlements in a foreign land. This was done at the expense of the original inhabitants who were often killed, enslaved or displaced.

Conakry: (KAHN uh kree) The capital city of Guinea.

Cote d'Ivoire: (KOHT D'Voir) A former colony of France located on the western border of Ghana. Also referred to as Ivory Coast.

Council of Elders: Groups of advisors to an African village chief, who make decisions which affect the village.

Cudjoe: (Coo JOE) A great African who became the military leader of the Maroons in Jamaica in their war of liberation against the British.

Dakar: (dah KAHR) The capital city of Senegal.

Descendant: An individual who is an offspring of their ancestors.

Diop, Cheikh Anta: *(SHAKE An ta DEE Op)* A Senegalese born scientist, politician and Egyptologist. He was voted one of the most influential scholars of the 20th century on the African world.

Diop, Cheikh Anta University: Formerly known as the University of Dakar, it is Senegal's only university and was renamed in honor of Cheikh Anta Diop.

Door of no return: Door through which enslaved Africans walked when leaving the slave dungeons before boarding the slave ships which would take them to America.

Drinking Gourd: A term used by enslaved Africans to describe the Big Dipper.

Du Bois, W.E.B.: (do BOYZ) An African American born scholar and activist. DuBois moved to Ghana in 1961 and was a leader in the Pan Africanist movement.

DuSable, Jean Baptiste Pointe: (du SAH bul) Founder of the city of Chicago, IL.

DuSable Museum of African American History: A museum in Chicago, founded by Dr. Margaret Burrroughs and her husband Charles, in 1961. The museum was created to preserve the history and culture of African Americans for future generations.

Elders: Senior members of a community who have achieved status because of their age and wisdom.

Elmina: (EL Me Na) The site of a fort built by the Portuguese in 1482 in the central region of the Gold Coast (Ghana). Elmina means "The Mine."

Elmina Dungeon: One of the largest slave dungeons and forts in West Africa.

Equator: An imaginary line which divides the earth into a northern and southern hemisphere.

European Slave Trade: A term used to describe the enslavement of Africans by Europeans.

Fanti: (Fan ti) Member of an ethnic group inhabiting the coastal area of Ghana.

Fort James: A fort built on James Island to protect British merchants who participated in the slave trade.

Garvey, Marcus: Jamaican born organizer and advocate of economic and political independence for Africans at home and abroad.

Gerima, Haile: (HY lee GE ree MA) Ethiopian born filmmaker who wrote and directed the film *Sankofa*.

Gold Coast: The former name of a British colony in West Africa now known as Ghana. It is bordered by Ivory Coast on the West and Togo on the East.

Goree Island: (GOR ee) A slave dungeon built by the Portuguese off the coast of Dakar, Senegal. It is believed to be the departure point for the largest number of enslaved Africans.

Greenfield, Eloise: African American poetess and author of numerous children's books.

Griot: (GREE oh) A person who tells the oral history of the inhabitants of a village. A storyteller.

Guinea: (Gin ee) A West African coastal nation which borders Senegal to the Northeast and Ivory Coast to the Southwest.

Haiti: (HEY tee) A small Caribbean Island formerly known as Saint Dominique. Haiti was once a colony of France.

Haley, Alex: African American writer who was born in Henning, TN. His award winning publication, *"Roots"* traced his heritage back to his distant relative Kunta Kinte who was kidnapped in The Gambia and enslaved in the United States of America.

Houphouet-Boigny, Felix: ( OO FWAY bwah NYEE) The first President of Ivory Coast.

Imhotep: (im HO'tep) An architect, engineer, poet, physician and designer of the step pyramid in Egypt. He is often referred to as the world's first multi-genius.

Ivory Coast: An African country on the Western border of Ghana.

James Island: An island and slave fortress located on the Gambian River. Both were named after King James of England.

Jawara, Dawda Kairaba: (Da da Ka-Ra Ba JaWor A) Former President of The Gambia who was deposed in 1994.

Juffere: (JU fur ay) A tiny village in The Gambia. The home of Kunta Kinte, an ancestor of Alex Haley.

KKK: (Ku Klux Klan ) A racist group of White Supremacists which was founded around 1866 to oppress recently emancipated African Americans.

Kemet: (KIM' et) The original name of the North African country now referred to as Egypt.

Kente Cloth: (KIN tay) Beautiful woven strips of delicately embroidered fabric. The strips are sewn together to make colorful garments. Kente cloth is manufactured in central Ghana.

Kinte, Binta: (Ben TA KIN Tay) A distant cousin of Kunta Kinte and Alex Haley. She lives in the village of Juffere.

Kinte, Kunta: (KOON Ta KIN Tay) The great, great, great, great, great-grandfather of Alex Haley who was born in The Gambian village of Juffere around 1751. He was enslaved and brought to Annapolis, MD in 1767.

Kizzy: Daughter of Kunta Kinte.

Kunjunfu, Dr. Jawanza: (JA Wonza KUN Ju fu) A prominent African American author and educator.

Legon: (LAY gun) The campus of the University of Ghana located in a suburb of Accra.

Louisiana Purchase: The sale of the Louisiana Territory from France to the United States in 1803. The real estate transaction nearly doubled the size of the United States.

L'Ouverture, Toussaint: (Too SAN loo vehr TOOR) A brilliant military leader who became governor of Haiti after defeating the French colonists. The island of Haiti was formerly known as Saint Dominique.

Lynching: To kill by mob action without lawful trial.  A hanging.

Maafa: (MA a FA) A Kiswahili word which means "great disaster."  The term was first used by Dr. Marimba Ani to describe the European Slave Trade and its affect on enslaved Africans.

Maroon: A name given to the Africans who escaped from slavery.  It is a Spanish word which was also used to describe horses that have escaped to the wild.

Middle Passage: The Trans-Atlantic journey of the slave ships from West Africa to the West Indies or the Americas.

National Association of Black Social Workers: An association of African American Social Workers which was formed in 1968.

National Council for Black Studies: An organization formed by African American scholars in 1975 to formulate and stabilize the newly developed discipline of Black Studies.

Ndiaye, Joseph: (N JIA) Curator of the "House of Slaves" at Goree Island in Senegal.

Negro:  A Portuguese term used to describe people of African descent.  The word means "black" in Portuguese.

New World: The lands discovered by European explorers in the late 15th century.  It refers to North and South America and the Caribbean Islands, which was new to them.

Nkrumah, Kwame: (KWAH meh en KROO mah) Ghana's first Prime Minister who was elected President in 1960.  He led Ghana to independence against the British Colonists in 1957.

North Star:  (See *Polaris*)

Oguaa: (OH goo a) The indigenous name of the city of Cape Coast, in the central region of Ghana.

Oral History: The spoken history of  a group of people.

Pagans: A demeaning term used by members of a particular religion to describe people of a different religion.

Plantation: A large farm or estate where enslaved Africans were forced to work.

Playing the dozens: A game of verbal jousting in which players attempt to humiliate each other into submission.

Polaris: (PO lar is) The bright star almost directly above the northern end of the earth's axis; the polestar. It is often called the North Star.

Pope John Paul II: The current Spiritual leader of the Catholic Church.

Prosser, Gabriel: An African freedom fighter who planned a rebellion in Virginia in the early 1800's. The plotters of the insurrection were betrayed before their plans were implemented.

"Roots": The international best selling autobiography by Alex Haley.

Sahara: World's largest desert, covering two fifths of the northern portion of the continent of Africa. Arabic word for desert.

Saint Dominique: An island in the Caribbean now known as Haiti.

Sankofa: (SAN Koe fa) The process of returning to the past to gather information which is vital to your future development.

Savanna: Grassland, or bush. Over two fifths of Africa is savanna.

Seasoning: A term used by enslavers to describe the process of mentally and physically beating newly enslaved Africans into submission.

Senegal: (sehn uh GAWL) West African country which was formerly colonized by the French. It is bordered by Mauritania to the North and Guinea to the South.

Sierra Leone: (sih AIR uh lee OHN) A former French colony in West Africa which is bordered by Guinea to the North and Liberia to the South.

Slave: A person forced to provide free labor for an enslaver for an indefinite period of time.

Slave trade: (See *European Slave Trade*)

Soweto: (SO WAY TOE) A sprawling township in South Africa, located Southwest of Johannesburg.

Soweto Square: A monument in Dakar, Senegal, built in solidarity with the people of South Africa.

The Gambia: A former colony of Britain which was originally carved out of the nation of Senegal.

The Gambia River: One of the major waterways in The Gambia.

Toby: The name given Kunta Kinte after he was sold to a Virginia farmer.

Treichville: (TRYCH vil) An impoverished section of Abidjan, West Africa.

Tubman, Harriet: An African American freedom fighter who escaped from the South and served as a conductor on the Underground Railroad. She was responsible for liberating over 300 enslaved Africans.

Turner, Nat: An African American freedom fighter from Virginia who led a revolt which resulted in the death of dozens of European Americans.

Underground Railroad: A network of abolitionists who established safe havens for enslaved Africans who journeyed from the South into the free states of the North and Canada.

University of Dakar: (See *Cheikh Anta Diop University*)

University of Ghana: The national university of Ghana which has campuses in Legon and Cape Coast. The University of Science and Technology is located in the city of Kumasi. (See *Legon*)

Wolof: (Woo lof) Primary language spoken by Africans in Senegal.

Yanga: An enslaved African in Mexico who led a group of Maroons in a war of liberation against the Spanish around 1612. He later became governor of the town which bears his name.

Zong: A British slave ship from which 132 Africans were thrown overboard in 1781.

# Index

Items in text are in regular print
Margin notes are in **boldface**
Illustrations and photos are in **(parenthesis)**

# Suggested Readings

Akbar, Na'im, *Chains and Images of Psychological Slavery,* New
Mind Productions, Tallahassee, FL, 1984.

Anyike, James C., *African American Holidays*, Popular Truth,
Chicago, IL, 1991.

Browder, Anthony T. , *From The Browder File: 22 Essays On The
African American Experience*, The Institute of Karmic Guidance,
Washington, DC,  1989.
\_\_\_\_, and Atlantis Tye, *My First Trip To Africa*, The Institute of
Karmic Guidance, Washington, DC, 1991.
\_\_\_\_, *Nile Valley Contributions To Civilization*, The Institute of
Karmic Guidance, Washington, DC, 1992.

Clarke, John Henrik, *African People in World History*, Black
Classic Press, Baltimore, MD, 1993.

Cowan, Tom & Maguire, Jack, *Timelines Of African-American
History: 500 Years of Black Achievement*, The Berkley Publishing
Group, New York, NY, 1994.

Everett, Susanne, *History of Slavery*, Chartwell Books, Inc.,
Secaucus, NJ, 1994.

Feelings, Tom, *The Middle Passage: White Ships/Black Cargo,*
Dial Books, 1995

Hilliard, Asa G., *The Maroon Within Us*, Black Classic Press,
Baltimore, MD, 1995.

Kafele, Baruti K., *A Black Parent's Handbook To Educating Your
Children (Outside of the Classroom)*, Baruti Publishing,
Jersey City, NJ, 1991.

Kitwana, Bakari, *The Rap On Gangsta Rap*, Third World Press,
Chicago, IL, 1994.

Kunjufu, Jawanza, *Developing Positive Self-Images & Discipline In
Black Children*, African American Images, Chicago, IL.

Leslau, Charlotte and Wolf, *African Proverbs*, Peter Pauper Press, Inc., White Plains, NY, 1962, 1985.

Madhubuti, Haki R, *Black Men: Obsolete, Single, Dangerous? African American Families in Transition*, Third World Press, 1990.

McWhorter, Abner, *An Introduction To Business For African American Youth*, Xpression Publishing, Detroit, MI, 1995.

Richards, Dona Marimba, *Let The Circle Be Unbroken*, The Red Sea Press, Trenton, NJ, 1980.

Walker, Wyatt Tee, The Soul of Black Worship, Martin Luther King Fellows Press, NY, NY, 1984.

Woodson, Carter G., *Mis-Education Of The Negro*, Associated Publishers, Washington, D.C., 1969.

Two sources of video and audio tapes which you should also investigate are:

To order VHS tapes of *Sankofa*, the soundtrack or other paraphernalia, contact:

**MYPHEDUH FILMS**
P.O. Box 10035, Washington, D.C. 20018-0035
(202) 289-6677 voice / (202) 289-4477 fax / 1-800-524-3895, e-mail: sankofa@cais.com

To order video tape interviews of African scholars, and audio tapes, publications, and posters of cultural literature, contact:

**SEAMON PUBLICATIONS**
579 Boney Road, Blythewood, SC, 29016
(803) 754-8472.

# End Notes

The Ghanaian proverb which states, *"The ruin of a nation begins in the homes of its people"* provides a simple solution for many of the problems which confront us today.  That is; the salvation of a nation *begins* in the homes of its people. In order to survive, within a sick nation, every family must be inoculated against the illnesses which exist within the society.

Prior to our departure to West Africa, we were advised to take several shots, and a weekly malaria tablet.  Those steps were necessary to protect us while we visited the continent. I now realize that throughout our trip we were constantly being given injections of history and culture in order to protect us when we returned to the United States.

The co-authoring relationship that exists between my daughter and me is the result of a commitment we made years ago.  We agreed to write books about our travels and deposit the revenue generated, from book sales and speaking engagements, in a trust fund to pay for her college education.

I immunized Atlantis once to protect her from childhood diseases.  I've immunized her again (and given her regular booster shots) in an attempt to protect her from the diseases of racism and mental slavery which she will be exposed to all of her adult life.

I believe that it is the responsibility of all parents to devise a methodology for the wholesome development of their offspring.  Children must be raised in an environment where their physical needs are met and where they are also given a value system which sustains their mental and spiritual growth and development.

In order to bring out the best in our children we must teach them to value their history and culture.  We must use every opportunity available to us to shift their focus from entertainment to education and teach them to become critical thinkers and designers of their own future.

Every home should have a collection of books by and about people of African descent and time should be established for regular discussions of issues that are critical to our survival. Since television plays a prominent role in most households, you should also establish a video tape library of programs that will enhance your child's well-being. I'm not talking about *Pocahontas* or *The Lion King*, but movies and programs of substance that will enhance your child's awareness of reality.

Music has also played a critical role in the lives of youth and teenagers, but they must be taught to understand how it affects their behavior. They must learn to hear the "message in the music" and not just to respond to the beat. They should be taught to appreciate a variety of musical expressions, because a child can't live by Rap alone.

The music of the past has value. The "oldies" that are being "sampled" and revised by so many young musicians are actually reconnecting them to our past. This is an act of "Sankofa" which builds an intergenerational bridge between the old and new forms of music. You can take advantage of this opportunity and discuss the concepts of Sankofa as you listen to the original tunes and contrast them with the new ones. This Sankofa principle applies to many aspects of life.

There is also a great need to patronize the cultural institutions within our communities. The libraries and museums in your city are paid for by our tax dollars and they are warehouses of information which are often underutilized by those who need them the most.

Lastly, be aware that travel is one of the best educational experiences one can ever have. The excitement of preparing for a journey and meeting new people stays with you for a lifetime. It also brings joy to those with whom you share your experiences. It doesn't matter if you travel across the world, across town or across the street. There are numerous opportunities awaiting you. They are experiences which will allow you to learn, grow and teach -- take advantages of them and teach your children to appreciate the wonders that the world has to offer.

## My First Trip To Africa
by Atlantis Tye Browder
with Anthony T. Browder

#200  Paperback  $ 8.95
#201  Hardcover  $16.95

**My First Trip To Africa** chronicles the experiences of 7-year-old Atlantis Browder during a 13-day study tour to Egypt in November 1989.  This 40 page book contains 27 photographs, 15 illustrations 3 maps, a glossary and a parent /teacher guide.

## Africa On My Mind:
## Reflections Of My Second Trip
by Atlantis Tye Browder
with Anthony T. Browder

#202  Paperback  $11.99
#203  Hardcover  $24.99

**Africa On My Mind** chronicles the experiences of 11-year-old Atlantis Browder during a 15-day study tour to the West African nations of Senegal, The Gambia, Ghana and Ivory Coast.  The final chapter consists of a conversation between Atlantis and her dad as they discuss the relevancy of her trip.  This 104 page book contains 47 photographs, 18 illustrations, 9 maps, 2 charts, a glossary, an index and a list of suggested readings.

## From The Browder File:
### 22 Essays On The African American Experience

## Exploding The Myths Vol. 1
### Nile Valley Contributions To Civilization

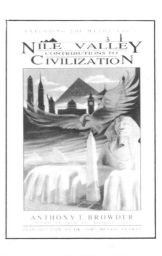

A compilation of essays exploring a myriad of topics ranging from African history and religion to eating habits, hairstyles and parental responsibility.

| | | |
|---|---|---|
| #100 | Paperback | $10.00 |
| #100A | Audio Cassette | $15.00 |
| #100B | Book & Cassette | $23.00 |

An in-depth examination of Nile Valley (Egyptian) civilization and its influence in the development of contemporary culture. The text is beautifully illustrated with numerous photographs, illustrations, maps and charts.

| | | |
|---|---|---|
| #100C | Paperback | $16.95 |
| #100D | Hardcover | $39.95 |

## ORDER FORM

| Item No. | Quantity | Description | Price Per Item | Total Price |
|---|---|---|---|---|
| | | | | |
| | | | | |
| | | | | |
| | | | | |

Subtotal: $_____

Shipping/Handling ($4.00 per 1st item and $2.00 per each additional item): $_____

Total: $_____

Name _____

Address _____ City _____

State _____ Zip _____ Telephone (_____) _____

Make check payable to: **The Institute of Karmic Guidance**
PO Box 73025 * Washington, DC 20056 * (301) 853-2465 * Fax: 301/853-7916

| To Charge Your Purchase: |
|---|
| Check One:     ( ) MASTERCARD          ( ) VISA          ( ) AMERICAN EXPRESS |
| CARD #_____     Exp. Date_____ |
|                                                                                                    Month / Year |
| X_____ |
| Signature required only if charging your purchase |

### THANK YOU FOR YOUR ORDER

* Please call or write for catalog of additional audio and video tapes *

# About the Authors

**Atlantis Tye Browder** is 13 years old and lives in suburban Washington, D.C. with her dad and grandmother. She is Vice President of her 8th grade class at G. E. Peters Elementary School in Hyattsville, MD.

In 1989, Atlantis went to Egypt on a Study Tour with her father, grandmother and 31 other people. During the summer of 1993, she travelled to Senegal, The Gambia, Ghana and The Ivory Coast in West Africa.

In February 1991 she and her father co-authored a book entitled *My First Trip To Africa*. This book chronicles Atlantis' visit to Egypt. This, her second book, *Africa On My Mind: Reflections Of My Second Trip* chronicles her visit to West Africa.

Atlantis has shared her travel experiences with audiences through out the United States and in Manchester England. She has appeared on Black Entertainment Television and WHMM-TV in Washington, D.C., and has conducted many radio and print interviews.

In April 1994, Atlantis and her father traveled to Manchester, England where they both participated in the Education of the Black Child Conference at Manchester University. She and her dad expect to write a series of books about her travels throughout the world.


**Anthony T. Browder** is a native of Chicago, Illinois and a graduate of Howard University's College of Fine Arts. He is an author, publisher, cultural historian, graphic artist and an educational consultant. He lectures extensively on topics pertaining to African and African American History and Culture. He has lectured throughout the United States and in Mexico, Africa, Japan and Europe.

Mr. Browder is the founder and director of the Institute of Karmic Guidance, a culturally oriented organization which is dedicated to the positive portrayal of the worldwide African experience. Through the Institute, Mr. Browder sponsors lectures and seminars, conducts African-Centered tours of Washington, DC, publishes his research and personally escorts study tours to Egypt and West Africa.

Mr. Browder is the author and publisher of *From The Browder File: 22 Essays on the African American Experience* and *Exploding the Myths, Volume 1: Nile Valley Contributions To Civilization*. Mr. Browder's publications are currently being used in classrooms throughout the United States, and in Japan and England.